EMERGENCY
first response®

EMERGENCY FIRST RESPONSE®

This Participant Manual belongs to _____

Mailing Address _____

City _____ State/Province _____

Zip/Postal Code _____ Country _____

Phone Number _____

Instructor Statement

This person has completed the following Emergency First Response course requirements and indicated recommended skills.

☐ **Primary Care (CPR)**

Instructor Signature _____ Number _____

Completion Date _____

　☐　Optional Skill – Automated External Defibrillator (AED) Use

　☐　Optional Skill – Emergency Oxygen Use

☐ **Secondary Care (First Aid)**

Instructor Signature _____ Number _____

Completion Date _____

Emergency First Response® (EFR®)
Primary Care and Secondary Care Participant Manual

COPYRIGHT © 2011 by Emergency First Response Corp.

All rights reserved. Produced by Emergency First Response, Corp.
No reproduction of this book is allowed without the express written
permission of the publisher.

Published and distributed by Emergency First Response Corp.,
30151 Tomas, Rancho Santa Margarita, CA 92688-2125.
Printed in the United States of America.

ISBN number 978-1-61381-991-3
Product No. 70370 (6/11) Version 1.0

ACKNOWLEDGMENTS

For More Information

For more information about Emergency First Response, Corp., courses, products and emergency care go to www.emergencyfirstresponse.com.

Patient Care Standards

Emergency First Response Primary Care (CPR) and Secondary Care (First Aid) courses follow the emergency considerations and protocols as developed by the members of the International Liaison Committee on Resuscitation (ILCOR). Members include American Heart Association (AHA), European Resuscitation Council (ERC), Australian Resuscitation Council (ARC), New Zealand Resuscitation Council (NZRC), Heart and Stroke Foundation of Canada (HSFC), Resuscitation Council of Southern Africa (RCSA), Inter American Heart Foundation (IAHF), Resuscitation Council of Asia (RCA – current members include Japan, Korea, Singapore, Taiwan). Source authority for the development of content material in Emergency First Response programs is based on the following:

- Circulation, Journal of the American Heart Association. Volume 122, Number 18, Supplement 3. November 2010. http://circ.ahajournals.org/content/vol122/18_suppl_3/

- Resuscitation, Journal of the European Resuscitation Council. Volume 81, Number 1. October 2010. http://www.resuscitationjournal.com/

- Australian Resuscitation Council Guidelines. December 2010. http://www.resus.org.au/policy/guidelines/index.asp.

- New Zealand Resuscitation Council Policies and Guidelines. December 2010. http://www.nzrc.org.nz/policies-and-guidelines/.

Emergency First Response gratefully acknowledges the following contributors for their assistance with publishing this manual:

International Medical Review

Dr. Phil Bryson, MBChB, DCH, DRCOG, MRCGP

Medical Director of Diving Services
Abermed Ltd, Aberdeen

Des Gorman, BSc, MBChB, FAFOM, PhD

Head - Occupational Medicine
School of Medicine, University of Auckland
Auckland, New Zealand

Heidi Kapanka, MD, MPH

Emergency Medicine
Alabama, USA

Jan Risberg, MD, PhD

Begen, Norway

Brian Smith, MD

Mountain West Anesthesia
Utah, USA

Equipment

Laerdal Medical Corporation

Cardiac Science Corporation

Agilent/Phillips

HeartSine® Technologies, Incorporated

MIX
Paper from
responsible sources
FSC® C004755
www.fsc.org

About this **Manual**

The *Emergency First Response Participant Manual* has three sections

▶ **Section One – Independent Study Workbook**

▶ **Section Two – Skills Workbook**

▶ **Section Three – Emergency Reference**

Section One provides you with foundational information specific to Emergency Responder care. By reading the background information in this section, you'll better understand emergency care procedures and why your role as an Emergency First Responder is so important to those who need emergency care.

Section Two applies to the skill development portion of your Emergency First Response course. Under your Instructor's supervision, you'll use this step-by-step workbook to guide you through a practice session for each of the course's skills.

Section Three provides a quick emergency care reference to use after you complete your course. This section includes emergency care reference for:

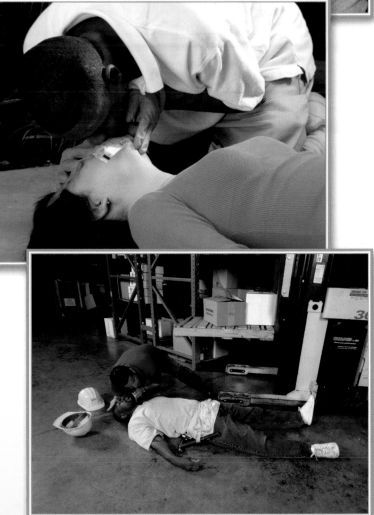

◆ Primary Care – CPR for Adults, Children and Infants

◆ Assembling a First Aid Kit

◆ Injury First Aid – Dislocations, fractures, cuts, scrapes, bruises, dental injuries, strains, sprains, eye injuries and electrical injuries

◆ Temperature-Related Injuries – Burns, hypothermia, frostbite, heat stroke and heat exhaustion

◆ Illness First Aid – Heart attack, stroke, diabetic problems, seizures, allergic reactions, poisoning, venomous bites and stings

Section ONE

Independent STUDY

Contents

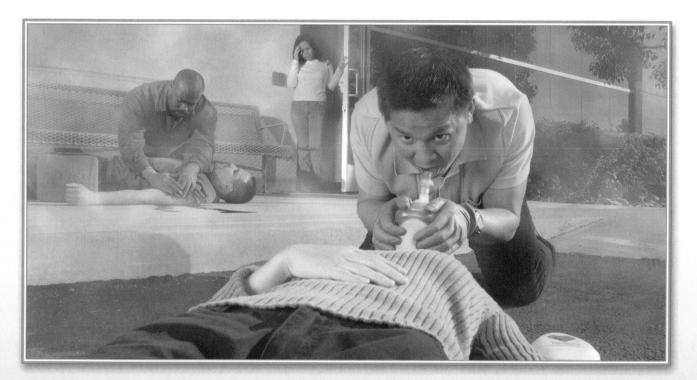

Section ONE

Independent Study

Introduction

Someone cuts his finger in a kitchen. At a gym, an older gentleman collapses from a heart attack. During a sporting event, a young boy faints from standing too long. Two automobiles collide, seriously injuring the occupants. A youngster floats motionless, face down in a swimming pool. A diner at the next table chokes on food, unable to breathe.

It happens every day. Some of these people just need a helping hand while others will die or suffer serious permanent injury if not immediately attended to. Many things separate those who live and escape serious disability from those who die or suffer long after their misfortune: the individual's fitness and health, the severity of the initial incident, the distance from medical care and often, just plain luck. No one can control these variables.

But there's one variable you *can* control when you're on the scene of any medical emergency: *You*. Often, life versus death or complete recovery versus long-term disability lies with a layperson first responder providing care between the emergency's onset and the arrival of professional medical personnel. If you are there, you can provide that care. *You* can be an Emergency Responder. As a layperson, you can't guarantee that a patient will live or fully recover — there's too much beyond anyone's control — but you can feel confident that given the circumstances, everything that could be done will be done.

If you're not familiar with emergency care procedures, it can seem intimidating and complex. What do you do? For that matter, how do you know what to do first? Such questions may appear overwhelming, but actually, they're not. If you can remember a simple memory word, you'll know what to do. This is because no matter what the nature of a medical emergency, you follow the same steps in the same order, providing basic care based on what you find. In the Emergency First Response Primary Care (CPR) and Secondary Care (First Aid) courses, you'll learn to follow the necessary steps in the right order, so you do the right things at the right time. You'll learn to apply first responder care following the same priorities used by medical professionals.

Regional Resuscitation Councils and Organizations

▶ American Heart Association (AHA) guidelines are used in Americas, United States, Canada, Asia and the Pacific Island countries.

▶ European Resuscitation Council (ERC) guidelines are used in the UK, Europe, Africa, Middle East and Russia.

▶ Australia and New Zealand Resuscitation Councils (ARC/NZRC) guidelines are used in Australia and New Zealand.

Significant regional differences in primary or secondary care are indicated by references to AHA, ERC or ARC/NZRC guidelines.

As a lay Emergency Responder, you'll learn to apply care following the same priorities used by medical professionals.

The *Cycle of Care*

Emergency First Response Primary Care (CPR) teaches you the steps and techniques for handling life-threatening emergencies. The *Cycle of Care* guides you.

> The Cycle of Care illustrates the correct pathway and priorities for emergency care.

Cycle of Care: AB-CABS™

Continue Until Help or AED Arrives

A B
Airway **B**reathing
Open? Normally?

C **C**hest **C**ompressions

A **A**irway Open

B **B**reathing for Patient

S **S**erious Bleeding **S**hock **S**pinal Injury

Check Quickly

Unresponsive & Not Breathing Normally

Responsive & Breathing Normally

The *Cycle of Care* illustrates the memory word AB-CABS, providing you with the correct pathway and priorities for emergency care. Visualize the *Cycle of Care* illustration as you assist someone in need. You continue a *Cycle of Care* for a patient until Emergency Medical Service personnel arrive and take over.

Primary Care Priorities: AB-CABS

A = Is the patient's **A**irway Open?

B = Is the patient **B**reathing Normally?

C = **C**hest **C**ompressions

A = Open **A**irway

B = **B**reathing for the Patient

S = **S**erious Bleeding, **S**hock, **S**pinal Injury

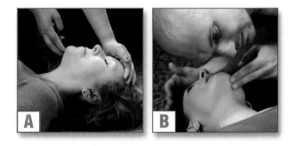

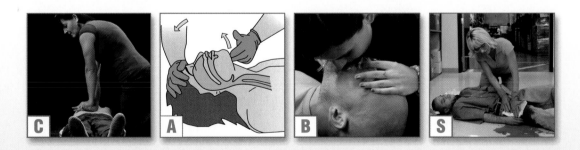

Course Structure

This manual and the *Emergency First Response Video* provide the study tools for two courses — Emergency First Response Primary Care (CPR) and Emergency First Response Secondary Care (First Aid). Your instructor may conduct these courses separately or together.

The Nine Skills Learned in Emergency First Response® Primary Care (CPR)

▶ Scene Assessment

▶ Barrier Use

▶ Primary Assessment

▶ CPR – Chest Compressions

▶ CPR – Chest Compressions Combined With Rescue Breathing

▶ Optional Skill — Automated External Defibrillator Use

▶ Serious Bleeding Management

▶ Shock Management

▶ Spinal Injury Management

▶ Conscious/Unconscious Choking Adult

▶ Optional Skill — Emergency Oxygen Use Orientation

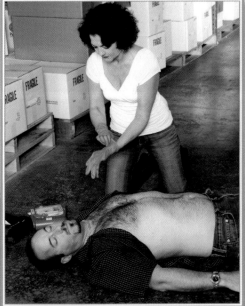

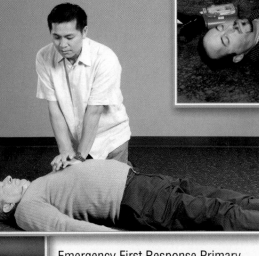

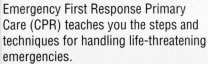

Emergency First Response Primary Care (CPR) teaches you the steps and techniques for handling life-threatening emergencies.

Emergency First Response Primary Care (CPR) teaches you the steps and techniques for handling life-threatening emergencies. In it, you'll learn nine skills for aiding patients who aren't breathing normally, have no heartbeat, may have serious bleeding, may be in shock or who may have a spinal injury. You'll learn how to apply the *Cycle of Care,* so that you provide the patient with every possible chance of survival in the face of the most serious emergencies.

The Four Skills Learned in Emergency First Response® Secondary Care (First Aid)

► Injury Assessment

► Illness Assessment

► Bandaging

► Splinting for Dislocations and Fractures

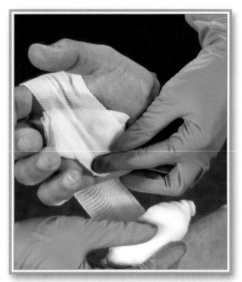

Emergency First Response Secondary Care (First Aid) teaches you what to do when Emergency Medical Services (EMS) are either delayed or unavailable. This course also teaches you how to provide first aid for patients with conditions that aren't life-threatening. You'll learn to apply the *Cycle of Care* in such a way to reduce imminent threats to a patient's life while providing care that reassures, eases pain and reduces the risk of further harm.

Emergency First Response Secondary Care (First Aid) teaches you what to do when Emergency Medical Services (EMS) are either delayed or unavailable.

For both courses, you'll begin by reading the Independent Study section of this manual and watching the *Emergency First Response Video.* This gives you the basic information about why each skill is important and how to do it. Then you'll practice the skill with your instructor so that you become capable and comfortable with it. After you've learned all of the skills in each course, your instructor will stage mock emergencies for you and your classmates. During these scenarios, you'll practice applying your skills and learn to adapt what you've learned to circumstances like you might find in real life. You'll find that the emphasis is on learning the skills so that you're comfortable using them.

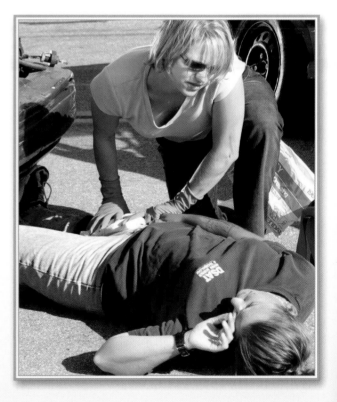

Additional EFR programs

Check with your Instructor for the availability of additional Emergency First Response programs in your region:

♦ Emergency First Response Refresher course

♦ Care for Children

♦ CPR & AED

♦ First Aid at Work

Course Flow – Begin Here

Read the Independent Study portion of this Participant Manual.

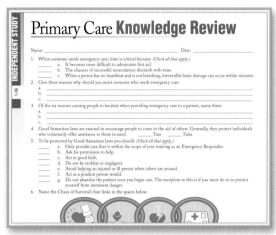

Complete the Knowledge Review at the end of the independent study portion of your Participant Manual.

Watch your *Emergency First Response Video.*

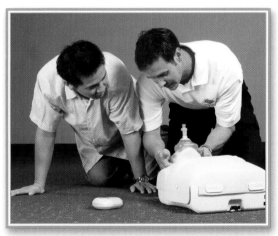

Attend the Skill Development session organized by your Emergency First Response Instructor.

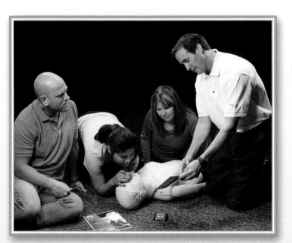

Complete the Scenario Practice with your Emergency First Response Instructor.

Learning Tips

Here are a few pointers to help you get the most out of the Emergency First Response Primary Care (CPR) and Secondary Care (First Aid) courses.

1. **Don't focus on perfection.** A common misconception with emergency care is that the smallest error will hurt or kill a patient. This is seldom true. Your instructor will make sure you understand what's critical and what's not. When someone focuses on perfection, there's a tendency to do nothing in a real emergency because that person fears not doing everything "perfectly." Don't get caught in that trap — it's not hard to provide adequate care. Always remember – *Adequate care provided is better than perfect care withheld.*

2. **Don't be intimidated.** You're learning something new, so don't be surprised if you're not immediately comfortable with a skill or need some guidance. Mistakes aren't a problem — they're an important part of learning.

3. **Have fun.** That may sound odd given the seriousness of what you're learning, but the truth is, you'll learn more and learn faster if you and your classmates keep things light. Polite humor and light jests are normal in this kind of learning. But, be sensitive and aware that others taking the course with you may have been involved in a situation similar to what you're practicing. You can have fun without seeming insensitive or uncaring about human suffering.

4. **Be decisive and then act.** There's more than one way to help a person that is injured or ill. When you practice the scenarios, you'll find that circumstances don't always give you a clear direction in exactly how to best apply the priorities of care.

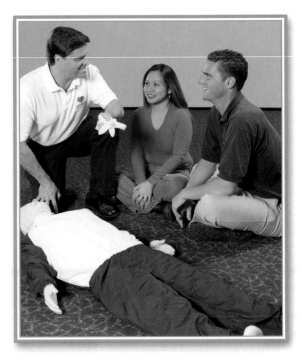

5. **It all comes back.** When you're practicing the scenarios, you may notice that as you follow the priorities of care explained in all Emergency First Response courses, the things you "forgot" come back to you — not necessarily smoothly at first, but adequately so that you're capable of providing emergency care. Remember that feeling. If you're ever faced with a real emergency and have doubts about remembering what to do, recall this feeling. Regardless of what you do or don't do, remember when helping someone in need that a*dequate care provided is better than perfect care withheld.*

6. **Complete all your independent study prior to class.** In most situations, your EFR Instructor will expect you to come to the Skill Development and Scenario Practice session having read all of your *Emergency First Response Participant Manual* and watched the entire *Emergency First Response Video*. Doing so will streamline your learning by allowing you to focus on skill development with your instructor. Begin by scanning a section, read through its study questions, then read the section. At the end of the independent study material, you will find one Knowledge Review for each course. Complete the Knowledge Review and bring it to class along with your participant manual.

Who May Enroll In Each Course and What Are The Prerequisites?

Anyone of any age may enroll in the Emergency First Response Primary Care (CPR) course. The course is performance-based, meaning that as long as you can meet each of the stated objectives and complete the necessary skills to the satisfaction of your instructor, you can receive a course completion card.

To enroll in the Emergency First Response Secondary Care (First Aid) course, you need only complete the Primary Care (CPR) course. Or, if you're currently CPR trained from another qualified training organization, you can enroll directly in the Emergency First Response Secondary Care (First Aid) course with a quick review by your instructor. Examples of other qualified CPR training organizations include: American Heart Association, Red Cross, American Safety and Health Institute, Cruz Roja de Mexico, Deutsches Rotes Kreuz, Medic First Aid, Inc®., Queensland Ambulance Service, South African Red Cross Society and St. John's Ambulance. There may be others that qualify; check with your instructor.

PARTICIPANT COMPLETION CARD
CPR/FIRST AID

Creating Confidence
to Care®

EMERGENCY
first response®

Helping Others in Need

If you encounter someone who needs primary emergency care and you've assessed the scene for your own personal safety (more on this later), you should render assistance immediately – even seconds count. The chances of successful resuscitation diminish with time. When a person has no heartbeat and is not breathing, irreversible brain damage can occur within minutes. Many medical emergencies, like sudden cardiac arrest, require the secondary assistance of Emergency Medical Service personnel. Get them on the scene fast - seconds count. It is typically best to alert the Emergency Medical Service first, before rendering emergency care (more on this later).

Besides providing an act of kindness toward a fellow human being in need, there are three basic reasons for assisting someone who needs emergency care:

1. You can save or restore a patient's life.

2. You can help reduce a patient's recovery time; either in the hospital or at home.

3. You can make the difference between a patient having a temporary or lifelong disability.

Some individuals, even when CPR and first aid trained, hesitate to provide emergency care to those in need. This is understandable and there are legitimate concerns on the part of Emergency Responders when helping those with injuries and illnesses. The six most common reasons why people hesitate to provide emergency care are:

1. **Anxiety.**

   People may hesitate due to general nervousness or anxiousness. This is a perfectly normal reaction when helping those in need. However, as it's been emphasized, trust your training. When you follow the priorities of care as outlined in this course, you are giving your patient the best chance for survival or revival.

2. **Guilt.**

   People may hesitate when thinking about how they might feel if the patient doesn't recover after delivering first aid. You can't guarantee that a patient will live or fully recover — there's too much beyond anyone's control. Be confident that any help you offer is a contribution to another human being and has the potential to make a difference in the patient's outcome. Even in the worst of outcomes, you can take comfort in the fact that you used your skills and gave the patient more of a chance than he had alone.

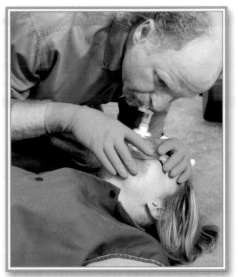

When someone is in need of emergency care, you should render assistance immediately – even seconds count.

3. **Fear of imperfect performance.**

People may hesitate because they feel they cannot properly help an injured or ill person. It is seldom true that the smallest error will hurt or kill a patient. During this course, you will learn what's critical and what's not. If you focus on perfection, you'll have a tendency to do nothing in a real emergency. Don't get caught in that trap — it's not hard to provide adequate care, and *adequate care provided is always better than perfect care withheld.*

4. **Fear of making a person worse.**

The most serious medical emergency is when a patient isn't breathing and has no heartbeat. Sometimes people hesitate to help such a patient, fearing they will make him worse. As an Emergency Responder, realize that you cannot make such a person worse. A person with no breathing and no heartbeat is already in the worst state of health. You can trust your training. Take a moment to relax, think of your training, then step forward and help.

5. **Fear of infection.**

People may hesitate because they are afraid of being infected by the person they are assisting. Keep in mind that a large percentage of all CPR is performed in the home or for a loved one or friend. In these cases, risk of infection is low and fear of infection should not cause you to withhold CPR or emergency care. Infection is a concern, but your training includes learning to use protective barriers to minimize the risk of disease transmission. By using barriers, you're highly unlikely to get any disease or infection from someone you help. Further, research has shown that the chance of disease transmission is very rare when providing CPR.

6. **Responsibility concerns.**

People may hesitate because they are afraid of being sued. In general, the fear of being sued should not stop Emergency Responders from providing emergency care. In many regions of the world, Good Samaritan laws have been put in place to encourage people to come to the aid of others.

Good Samaritan Laws

Good Samaritan laws (or related, local laws) are enacted to encourage people to come to the aid of others. In general, they protect individuals who voluntarily offer assistance to those in need. They are created to provide immunity against liability.

Often, a Good Samaritan law imposes no legal duty to help a stranger in need. However, local laws may vary on this point and in some areas people are required to provide aid. There may not be Good Samaritan laws in your local area. It would be wise to determine the extent and use of Good Samaritan laws in your local area. Your Emergency First Response Instructor may be able to provide you with information about Good Samaritan laws in your local region.

There are six ways you should act to be protected by Good Samaritan laws. They are:

1. Only provide care that is within the scope of your training as an Emergency Responder.

2. Ask for permission to help

3. Act in good faith.

4. Do not be reckless or negligent.

5. Act as a prudent person would.

6. Do not abandon the patient once you begin care. The exception to this is if you must do so to protect yourself from imminent danger.

Study Questions

◆ What is a Good Samaritan law?

◆ In general, what are the six ways you should act to be protected by most Good Samaritan laws?

Good Samaritan laws are enacted to encourage people to come to the aid of others.

The Chain of Survival and You - The Emergency Responder

The Chain of Survival illustrates the four links of patient care. It emphasizes the teamwork needed in emergency situations between you and professional emergency care providers. When you recognize a potentially life-threatening emergency, you help with the first three links in the Chain of Survival. The fourth link involves only professional emergency care providers – EMTs, Paramedics, nurses and doctors. Let's look at each of the four links in the Chain of Survival.

Study Question

◆ What are the Chain of Survival's four links and which three involve an Emergency Responder?

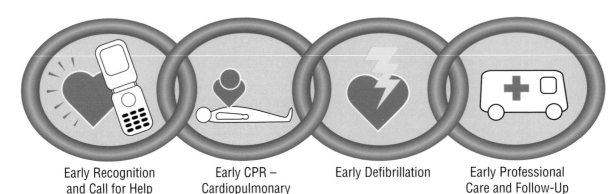

Early Recognition and Call for Help

Early CPR – Cardiopulmonary Resuscitation

Early Defibrillation

Early Professional Care and Follow-Up

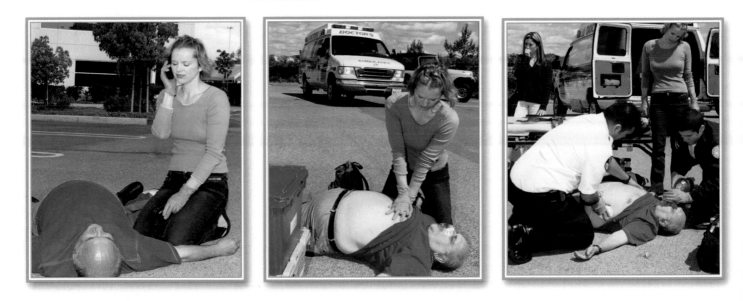

Early Recognition and Call for Help

As an Emergency Responder, you must first recognize that an emergency exists. Once you've determined that an emergency exists, evaluate the scene to determine if it is safe for you to assist the patient. You'll make sure a scene is safe by conducting a *Scene Assessment,* a skill you'll learn in the Emergency First Response Primary Care (CPR) course.

Further, for a patient with a life-threatening problem, you must rapidly activate the Emergency Medical Service (EMS) in your local area. This is the *Call First* concept. More on this to come.

Early CPR – Cardiopulmonary Resuscitation

A person who is not breathing normally and has no heartbeat needs CPR immediately. Early CPR is the best treatment for cardiac arrest until a defibrillator and more advanced trained professionals arrive. Effective and immediate chest compressions prolong the window of time during which defibrillation can occur and provides a small amount of blood flow to the heart, brain, and other vital organs. Immediate CPR can double or triple a patient's chance of survival from irregular heartbeats or sudden cardiac arrest. This link also involves you, the Emergency Responder.

Early Defibrillation

Combined with CPR, early defibrillation by you, the Emergency Responder, or EMS personnel, can significantly increase the probability of survival of a patient in cardiac arrest.

During your Primary Care course, you may learn how to use an Automated External Defibrillator (AED). If you witness a cardiac arrest and an AED is immediately available, you should begin chest compressions and use the AED as soon as possible (more on this later). When applied to a person in cardiac arrest, an AED automatically analyzes the patient's heart rhythm and indicates if an electric shock is needed to help restore a normal heartbeat. If you learn how to use an AED in this course, this link involves you, the Emergency Responder. Most EMS personnel also use AED units.

Early Professional Care and Follow-Up

EMS personnel can provide advanced patient care that you can not. The advanced care EMS personnel can provide includes artificial airways, oxygen, cardiac drugs and defibrillation (when an AED is unavailable).

After initial on-scene care, EMS personnel take the patient to the hospital for more advanced medical procedures. The patient remains hospitalized until no longer needing constant, direct medical attention.

Asking a Patient for Permission to Help

When an injured or ill responsive adult needs emergency care, ask permission before you assist the person. Asking for permission to help reassures the patient, noting that you are trained appropriately.

You ask for permission to help with the Responder Statement. You simply say, *Hello? My name is _____. I'm an Emergency Responder. May I help you?*

It's important to get the patient's agreement if he is alert and responsive. If the patient agrees or doesn't respond, you can proceed with emergency care. There is implied permission – meaning you can proceed with emergency care – if the patient is unresponsive. If an injured or ill responsive adult refuses emergency care, do not force it on the person. If possible, talk with the individual and monitor the patient's condition by observation without providing actual care. You could, however, activate EMS at this time.

Study Question
◆ How do you ask for permission to help a patient?

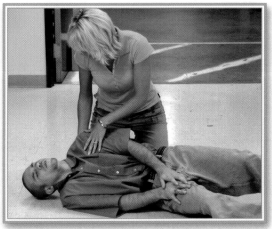

When an injured or ill responsive adult needs emergency care, ask permission before you assist the person. Asking for permission to help reassures the patient, noting that you are trained appropriately.

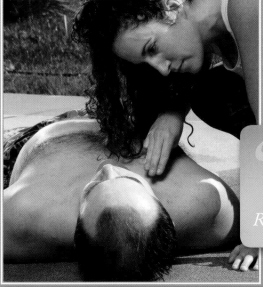

" Hello? My name is _____ I'm an Emergency Responder. May I help you?"

Activating the Emergency Medical Service – *Call First* and *Care First*

In the Chain of Survival your role as the Emergency Responder is to summon emergency medical aid and to assist the patient until it arrives. Activating EMS is so important that in most circumstances, if you're alone and there's no one else to activate the EMS for you, you *Call First*, then assist the patient.

After establishing patient unresponsiveness, and identifying that he is not breathing normally, ask a bystander to call EMS and secure an AED if possible. If you are alone, use your mobile phone to call EMS. If you do not have a mobile phone, leave the patient to call EMS if no other option exists. This is the *Call First* approach to emergency care. You *Call First* to activate Emergency Medical Services, then you provide assistance.

Study Questions

◆ When should you activate the Emergency Medical Service once you find an unresponsive adult or child who needs emergency care?

◆ How do you activate Emergency Medical Services (EMS) in your area?

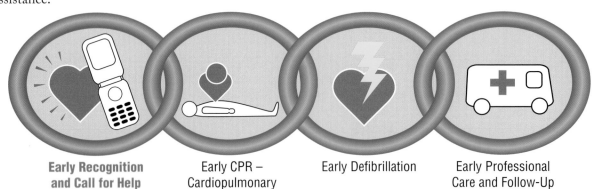

Early Recognition and Call for Help   Early CPR – Cardiopulmonary Resuscitation   Early Defibrillation   Early Professional Care and Follow-Up

An exception to the *Call First* rule is if the patient is a child or an adult who has experienced submersion in water. In these cases, you provide CPR for a *short time*, and then call EMS. This is called *Care First*.

> **NOTE** – Two national guidelines define providing *Care First* for a *short time* differently. In North, South and Central America, Asia and the Pacific Island countries (AHA Guidelines), it's defined as providing care for approximately 2 minutes; the European Resuscitation Council guidelines defines a short time as 1 minute.

With EMS on the way, the care you provide increases the chance that advanced care will help the patient when it arrives. Your training in this course is based on handling emergencies where you have an EMS system in place. If you need to provide emergency aid in areas away from EMS support, you should continue your education with more advanced first aid training.

> **NOTE** – You can dial 112 from any mobile cell phone anywhere in the world to reach EMS.

Call First means that if you're alone and there's no one else to activate the Emergency Medical Service for you, you *Call First*, then assist the patient.

In my local area, EMS is activated by calling: _____

The Emotional Aspects of Being an **Emergency Responder**

Helping another person in need is satisfying and feels good. Depending on the circumstances, however, it may also produce a certain amount of stress and some fearfulness. In most cases, a little stress may actually assist you when helping others by preparing you physically and mentally.

CPR – Cardiopulmonary Resuscitation – Is No Guarantee of a Successful Outcome

CPR is a two-step process - pressing on a patient's chest and breathing for the person. CPR is a temporary measure that can extend the window of opportunity for the patient to be revived.

CPR - and some types of first aid - are inherently emotional activities. However, as an Emergency Responder you should never fear harming a patient, especially when performing CPR on an individual who is unresponsive and not breathing normally. Why? Simply put - you really cannot make the person worse. A person that is unresponsive and not breathing normally is already in the worse state of health possible since he probably does not have a heartbeat.

If you perform CPR as outlined in this course, you really cannot make the patient worse than when you first found the individual. You don't need to fear providing CPR. Perform CPR to the best of your ability. Trust your training. If your efforts to revive a person in need do not succeed, focus on the fact that you tried your best to help.

But, if you could have provided CPR and didn't, you may spend the rest of your life wondering if it could have made a difference. Don't let that happen – again, trust your training. *Adequate care provided is better than perfect care withheld.*

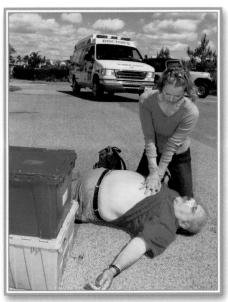

CPR - and some types of first aid - are inherently emotional activities. However, as an Emergency Responder you should never fear harming a patient when performing CPR on an individual who is unresponsive and not breathing normally.

Providing emergency care to those in need can be emotional. You may have elevated physical and emotional stress after providing emergency care. If you do, try the following:

▶ Try to relax after the incident. Lower your heartbeat and blood pressure by resting or walking slowly. Relaxing will reduce elevated adrenaline produced by your body to help you through the stress of providing emergency care.

▶ Avoid stimuli such as caffeine, nicotine or alcohol.

▶ Talk about the incident to others. Sharing your experience with others helps in processing thoughts and emotions, therefore reducing stress and anxiety. Talk can be a healing medicine.

▶ If you experience physical or emotional problems such as prolonged depression, sleeping disorders, persistent anxiety or eating disorders, seek the help of a health care professional.

▶ Spend time with others. Reach out – people care.

Responders In Action

As an Emergency Responder, if you provide care for an injured or ill person, we'd like to hear about it. Incidents need not be dramatic or involve a life-threatening condition. Sharing these stories not only encourages others to use their skills, but also helps monitor and gauge the effectiveness of Emergency First Response training and assists in future course development. Submit story online by going to www.emergencyfirstresponse.com.

Keeping Your Skills Fresh

When this course is completed, make it a point to practice your primary care skills from time to time. When not used or practiced, all skills deteriorate over time. CPR and first aid skills can begin to deteriorate as soon as six months after initial training.

Study Questions

♦ Why should you practice primary care skills after the course is over?

♦ How can you practice and refresh your skills?

Hopefully, you won't have to use your emergency skills in an actual situation. But even if you don't, you will still need to practice your skills to keep them fresh and properly sequenced. Everyone is nervous when they arrive on the scene of badly injured individuals. Practicing your skills and keeping them fresh in your mind will reduce your nervousness. You can review and practice your skills on your own by:

▶ Reviewing your *Emergency First Response Video.*

▶ Reading through this manual.

▶ Role-playing scenarios with your family members or friends.

▶ Walking through the CPR sequence using a pillow or appropriately-sized stuffed bag.

An easy and effective way to practice and fine-tune your emergency care skills is by enrolling in an Emergency First Response Refresher course. During the Refresher course, you'll practice your skills once again by completing the Skill Development portion of an EFR course with an Emergency First Response Instructor. After completing the refresher, you'll be issued a new Emergency First Response completion card. It's a good idea to take a Refresher course at least every 12 to 24 months to keep your skills and completion card current. Also, check with your Emergency First Response Instructor for any specific workplace or other local recertification requirements.

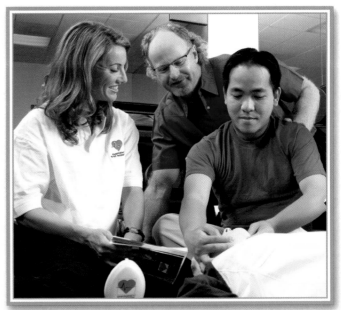

An easy and effective way to practice and fine-tune your emergency care skills is by enrolling in an Emergency First Response Refresher course.

Leading a **Healthy Lifestyle**

In many countries, more men and women die from coronary heart disease each year than from all other causes of death *combined*, including cancer and AIDS. It is fitting to discuss how you can reduce your own risk of coronary heart disease and lead a healthy lifestyle. Reducing your risk will also help you be a more fit Emergency Responder. Here are five ways you can reduce your risk of heart disease:

Study Questions

- What five ways can you keep your own heart healthy and avoid coronary heart disease?
- How can you lead an all-around healthy lifestyle?

▶ Avoid exposure to cigarette smoke.

▶ Reduce and manage stress.

▶ Eat a diet low in saturated fat, transfat, highly refined carbohydrates and cholesterol.

▶ Exercise regularly with your physician's guidance. To maintain a moderate level of fitness, health and fitness professionals recommend a minimum of 30 to 60 minutes of exercise, on most days of the week, at 50 to 80 percent of your maximum capacity. Your exercise should include resistance training and cardiovascular training for optimum health and fitness.

▶ If you have high blood pressure or diabetes, keep up with the treatment procedures agreed upon with your doctor. Both high blood pressure and diabetes are risk factors for heart disease. In general, get regular checkups by your physician.

There are other ways to lead an all-around healthy lifestyle. Consider the following:

▶ Learn to relax, but don't be lethargic.

▶ Manage stress. Don't merely focus on how to avoid it.

▶ Take care of yourself so you are able to function effectively as an Emergency Responder. Helping others in their time of need will put stress on your body – both emotionally and physically.

"Your exercise should include resistance training and cardiovascular training."

Protecting Yourself Against Bloodborne Pathogens

Infections (viruses, bacteria or other microorganisms) carried by the blood are called *bloodborne pathogens*. The three *bloodborne pathogens* of greatest concern to Emergency Responders are:

▶ Hepatitis C virus

▶ Hepatitis B virus

▶ Human immunodeficiency virus (HIV)

As an Emergency Responder, there are four ways you can protect yourself against *bloodborne pathogens* when assisting those in need of emergency care:

▶ Use gloves.

▶ Use ventilation masks or face shields when giving mouth-to-mouth rescue breathing.

▶ Use eye or face shields; including eye glasses or sunglasses, goggles and face masks.

▶ Always wash your hands or any other area with antibacterial soap and water after providing primary (CPR) and secondary (first aid) care. Scrub vigorously, creating lots of lather. If water is not available, use antibacterial wipes or soapless liquids.

As a general rule, always place a barrier between you and any moist or wet substance originating from a patient. All blood and body fluid should be considered potentially infectious. Take precautions to protect yourself against them.

As an Emergency Responder you will want to avoid infections by bloodborne pathogens. Fear of disease transmission is a common reason why laypersons trained in CPR avoid action. However, it is important to note that research has shown that chance of disease transmission is very rare when providing CPR. Do not delay emergency patient care if barriers are not available. If gloves and ventilation barriers are immediately available, use them during CPR to protect yourself and the patient from possible disease transmission. When available, use eye shields and facemasks when patients have serious bleeding.

Study Questions

◆ What three bloodborne pathogens are of greatest concern to Emergency Responders?

◆ As an Emergency Responder, what four ways can you protect yourself against bloodborne pathogens?

◆ As an Emergency Responder, what general rule may help you avoid infection by bloodborne pathogens?

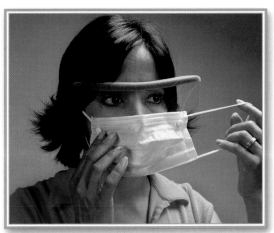

Use of barriers when providing emergency care can protect you against *bloodborne pathogens*. This photo shows a facemask with an attached eye shield.

Face Mask and Eye Shields

Gloves are easy to keep in your vehicle and on your person.

Recognizing Life-Threatening Problems

When you witness a serious car accident or watch someone take a bad fall, it's reasonable to assume the patient will have life-threatening injuries. Even if you don't see it occur, many accident scenes clearly point to medical emergencies.

Unfortunately, not all life-threatening emergencies are so obvious. Some serious conditions occur due to illness or subtle accidents. Sometimes the patient's symptoms come on quickly and other times the patient gets progressively worse over time. Because time is critical, as you've already learned, you need to be able to recognize all life-threatening conditions and then provide appropriate emergency medical care.

Study Question

◆ How can you recognize life-threatening emergencies like:

→ Heart attack

→ Cardiac arrest

→ Stroke

→ Complete/Severe airway obstruction

Heart Attack

A heart attack occurs when blood flow to part of the patient's heart is stopped or greatly reduced.

Heart attack patients commonly complain of chest pain and an uncomfortable pressure or squeezing. This usually lasts for more than a few minutes, or goes away and comes back. The pain is sometimes described as an ache, or feeling similar to heartburn or indigestion. Pain may spread to the shoulders, neck or arms. Patients may also complain of nausea, shortness of breath and dizziness or lightheadedness. They may sweat or faint.

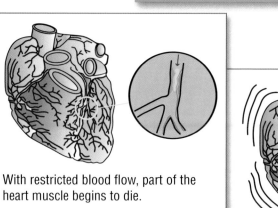

With restricted blood flow, part of the heart muscle begins to die.

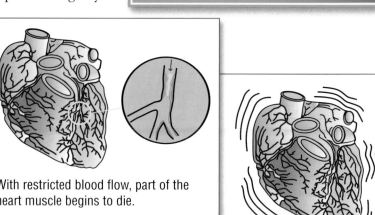

Ventricular fibrillation

Often, heart attack patients deny that anything is seriously wrong. This is especially true when symptoms are mild or go away temporarily. If you suspect a heart attack, do not delay calling EMS or transporting the patient to a medical facility. The longer the heart goes without adequate blood flow, the more permanent damage is likely to occur.

Cardiac Arrest

When a heart artery becomes blocked and the heart stops receiving oxygen, it may begin to quiver – called *ventricular fibrillation* – or just stop beating. This is called cardiac arrest. Although cardiac arrest is most often caused by heart disease or heart defects, it can occur any time regular heart rhythms are disturbed.

There are two ways to recognize cardiac arrest. First, the patient does not respond when you speak to or touch him. He is unresponsive. Second, the patient does not appear to have any signs of circulation – is not breathing normally, coughing, and is not moving. Beginning CPR immediately and providing defibrillation as quickly as possible are critical to patient survival.

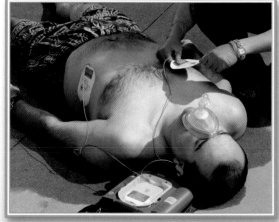

Beginning CPR immediately and providing defibrillation as quickly as possible are critical to patient survival.

Stroke

A stroke occurs when a blood vessel is blocked or ruptures in the patient's brain. Blockage or rupture deprives the brain of oxygen and causes cell death. Signs, symptoms and damage depend on which part of the brain is affected.

Use the memory word FAST to help you identify if a patient is having a stroke.

F = Face. Ask the patient to smile. Does one side of their face droop?.

A = Arms. Ask the patient to raise both arms. Does one arm drift downward?

S = Speech. Ask the person to repeat a simple phrase. Is their speech slurred or strange?

T = Time. If you observe any of these signs, call EMS immediately.

Common signs and symptoms of a stroke include:

1. Sudden weakness or numbness of the face, arm, or leg, especially on one side of the body or on both sides

2. Sudden confusion or drowsiness

3. Trouble speaking, understanding or swallowing

4. Sudden vision trouble from one or both eyes

5. Sudden trouble walking, dizziness, loss of balance or coordination

6. Sudden severe headache with no known cause

Some strokes are mild and last for only a few minutes while others are serious and debilitating. If you suspect a stroke, do not delay in calling EMS or transporting the patient to a medical facility. Mild strokes often precede more serious strokes, making immediate medical care crucial.

Early recognition and treatment of stroke helps minimize damage to the patient's brain.

Complete/Severe Airway Obstruction

Complete/Severe airway obstruction usually results when a patient chokes on food, although any object placed in the mouth could end up blocking the patient's airway. Recognizing airway obstruction is important because the patient can't speak. Patients also tend to become embarrassed and try to leave the area.

You may suspect choking if a patient grasps or clutches the neck or throat area. This is the universal distress signal for choking. By asking the patient what's wrong, you can determine if the patient can speak, is breathing or is able to cough. A patient with a complete or severe airway obstruction may become unconscious if the airway is not cleared quickly.

The universal signal for *"I am choking."*

During skill development, you will learn to help dislodge the obstruction and care for a choking patient.

Primary Care Definitions and Background Information

The Emergency First Response courses, Primary Care (CPR) and Secondary Care (First Aid), are skill intensive. However, skills alone are not enough. Knowing how, why and when to apply your skills during an emergency is important as well. The definitions and background information outlined here will give you the confidence to use your skills – knowing you are giving the correct care in the correct sequence.

Study Questions

♦ What is Primary Assessment and Primary Care?

♦ What does CPR stand for, what is it and how does it work?

♦ How do you determine if a person is unresponsive and not breathing normally?

♦ What causes a person to stop breathing?

♦ How does rescue breathing work?

Primary Assessment and Primary Care

Primary means *first in a series or sequence.* It means *most important.* An assessment is an *evaluation* or an *appraisal.* Therefore, in terms of emergency care, a *primary assessment* is an Emergency Responder's *first evaluation* of an injured or ill person. Primary assessment is the first step of emergency care.

Primary assessment also refers to the evaluation of a patient for *any* life-threatening conditions needing immediate attention – heart and breathing problems, choking, serious bleeding, shock and spinal injuries. You will be able to provide *primary care* to patients with these life-threatening injuries or illnesses. Injuries and illnesses that are life-threatening need to be treated first.

CPR

CPR stands for *Cardiopulmonary Resuscitation. Cardio* means "heart" and *Pulmonary* means "concerning the lungs and breathing." *Resuscitation* means "to revive from unconsciousness." If a patient is unresponsive and not breathing normally, you begin CPR immediately. We'll discuss what we mean by "not breathing normally" in just a bit.

C = CARDIO
"heart"

P = PULMONARY
"concerning the lungs – breathing"

R = RESUSCITATION
"to revive from unconsciousness"

As discussed earlier, CPR is a two-step process. First, press on a patient's chest and second, blow in the patient's mouth providing him oxygen. Complete CPR combines manual chest compressions with rescue breathing.

Primary assessment also refers to the evaluation of a patient for any life-threatening conditions needing immediate attention.

CPR is a two-step process. First, press on a patient's chest.

Second, blow in the patient's mouth.

How Does CPR Work

The heart pumps oxygen-rich blood throughout the body. It also returns the oxygen-poor blood to the lungs for more oxygen. If the heart is beating erratically or not beating at all, rescue breathing alone is ineffective. If a patient's heart has stopped, you substitute manual chest compressions for the heart's pumping action to circulate blood through the body.

Chest compressions force blood from the heart through the arteries and deliver oxygen-rich blood to vital organs. These manual chest compressions deliver no more than one third of normal blood flow to the body. Therefore, as an Emergency Responder you must begin compressions immediately and minimize interruptions during CPR. Delaying chest compressions for any reason is counterproductive.

CPR is used as an interim emergency care procedure until an AED and/or EMS personnel arrive. However, it is a vital link in the *Chain of Survival*.

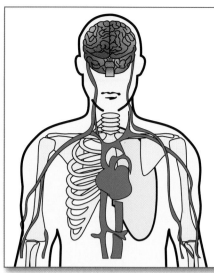

The heart pumps oxygen-rich blood throughout the body. It also returns the oxygen-poor blood to the lungs for more oxygen.

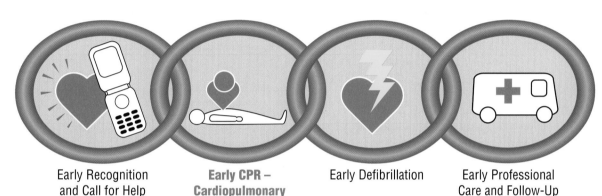

Early Recognition and Call for Help

Early CPR – Cardiopulmonary Resuscitation

Early Defibrillation

Early Professional Care and Follow-Up

"As an Emergency Responder you must begin compressions immediately and minimize interruptions during CPR."

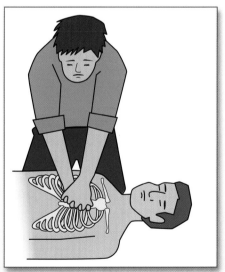

Chest compressions force blood from the heart through the arteries and deliver oxygen-rich blood to vital organs.

CPR extends the window of opportunity for resuscitation – greatly increasing the patient's chance of revival. That said, CPR rescue efforts are difficult to sustain for long periods. From an Emergency Responder perspective, CPR is exhausting. This is another reason to call the EMS immediately. To reduce fatigue, change rescuers every few minutes. Switching rescuers will reduce deterioration of chest compression quality.

Regarding CPR, if you are unable or feel uncomfortable giving a nonbreathing patient rescue breaths – RELAX! Simply give the patient continuous chest compressions. Chest compressions alone are very beneficial to a patient who is unresponsive and not breathing normally. Your efforts may still help circulate blood that contains some oxygen. Remember: *Adequate care provided is better than perfect care withheld.* You will learn adult CPR during your Primary Care Skill Development sessions.

Unresponsive Patients Who Are Not Breathing Normally

Unresponsive patients who are not breathing normally may be in cardiac arrest. Rapid recognition of cardiac arrest is very important. After you've determined that a patient is unresponsive and not breathing normally, activate EMS immediately. Next, you begin CPR.

What does *unresponsive* mean? A patient who is unresponsive shows no sign of movement and does not respond to stimulation, such as a tap on the collarbone or loud talking. This is also known as unconsciousness.

What does *not breathing normally* mean? An unresponsive person taking gasping breaths is NOT breathing normally. In the first few minutes after cardiac arrest, a patient may be barely breathing, or taking infrequent, slow and noisy gasps. Do not confuse this with normal breathing. A patient barely breathing, or taking infrequent, slow and noisy gasps needs CPR immediately.

How do you determine if an unresponsive person is breathing normally? Most unresponsive individuals in cardiac arrest will not be breathing at all. During the Primary Care Skill Development sessions you will learn how to quickly check a patient for responsiveness and normal breathing.

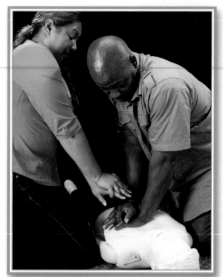

To reduce fatigue, change rescuers every few minutes. Switching rescuers will reduce deterioration of chest compression quality.

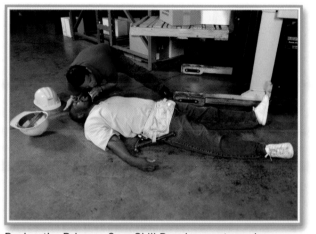

During the Primary Care Skill Development sessions you will learn how to quickly check a patient for responsiveness and normal breathing.

NOTE – Do not take time to check for a pulse. Studies show that even healthcare providers have difficulty detecting a pulse on unresponsive patients. Checking for a pulse takes too much time. Instead, immediately begin CPR.

"Regarding CPR, if you are unable or feel uncomfortable giving a nonbreathing patient rescue breaths – RELAX! Simply give the patient continuous chest compressions."

Reasons for a Person to Stop Breathing

A person may not be breathing for a number of reasons. Here are ten:

1. Heart attack or sudden cardiac arrest
2. Submersion and near drowning
3. Stroke
4. Foreign body airway obstruction – choking
5. Smoke inhalation
6. Drug overdose
7. Electrocution, suffocation
8. Injuries
9. Lightning strike
10. Coma

How Rescue Breathing Works

If after providing chest compressions to an unresponsive patient you decide to give him rescue breaths, there is plenty of unused oxygen in your expired breath to help a nonbreathing patient. The air we breathe contains 21 percent oxygen. We use about five percent for ourselves. This leaves a very high percentage of oxygen in the air we exhale after each breath. The unused oxygen can be used for rescue breathing to support a nonbreathing patient. You will learn how to perform and will practice giving rescue breaths in your Skill Development session.

> **NOTE** – If you are unable or feel uncomfortable giving an unresponsive patient rescue breaths – RELAX. Simply give the patient continuous chest compressions. Chest compressions alone are very beneficial to a patient without a heartbeat. Your efforts may still help circulate blood that contains some oxygen.

You will learn how to perform and will practice giving rescue breaths in your Skill Development session.

Using AB-CABS and the *Cycle of Care* to **Prioritize Primary Care**

Remembering How to Help

If you are ever in a situation where you can help another in need, nervousness will be natural. Your nervousness can make it difficult to remember what to do and how to do it. To help you remember what to do, the memory word (mnemonic) AB-CABS can be used to remind you of the pathway and priorities of emergency care. By learning this memory word, you'll know what to do first, second, third and so on when a person with a life-threatening illness or injury needs you. The meaning and prioritized flow of AB-CABS is:

Study Questions

- What does the AB-CABS memory word mean?
- What is meant by the *Cycle of Care*?
- What do you do if you discover a patient is not breathing normally?

A = **A**irway Open?

B = **B**reathing Normally?

C = **C**hest **C**ompressions

A = **A**irway Open

B = **B**reathing for the Patient

S = **S**erious Bleeding, **S**hock, **S**pinal Injury

Cycle of Care: AB-CABS™

Continue Until Help or AED Arrives

A B
Airway **B**reathing
Open? Normally?

C
Chest
Compressions

A **A**irway Open

B **B**reathing for Patient

S **S**erious Bleeding
Shock
Spinal Injury

Also Helping You Remember...

The first "A" in the memory word AB-CABS can mean more than simply asking the question is the patient's "**A**irway Open?" It can also remind you, in priority order, to **A**ssess the Scene for personal safety and **A**pply Barriers – gloves, ventilation shields, facemasks and eye shields. These are two of the first actions you complete before helping a person in need. You'll learn how to assess a scene and apply barriers during the skills portion of this course.

The AB-CABS *Cycle of Care* Graphic

When you first begin to assist a patient with a life-threatening illness or injury, reflect on the AB-CABS *Cycle of Care* graphic:

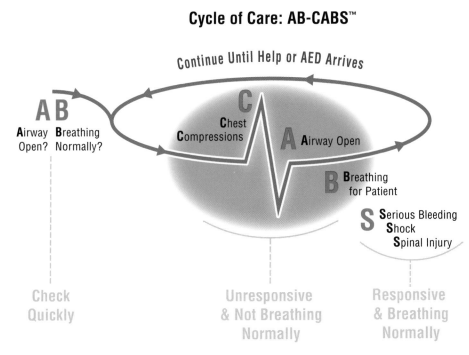

Cycle of Care: AB-CABS™

Continue Until Help or AED Arrives

A B
Airway Breathing
Open? Normally?

C Chest Compressions

A Airway Open

B Breathing for Patient

S Serious Bleeding
Shock
Spinal Injury

Check Quickly

Unresponsive & Not Breathing Normally

Responsive & Breathing Normally

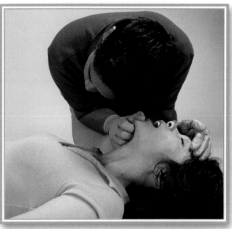

First begin with the "AB" portion of the memory word. This reminds you to quickly check to see if the patient's **A**irway is open and to note if he's **B**reathing normally.

Reading from left to right on the graphic you first begin with the "AB" portion of the memory word. This reminds you to quickly check to see if the patient's <u>A</u>irway is open and to check if he's <u>B</u>reathing normally. If his airway is open and he's not breathing normally, move to the "CAB" portion of the memory word (in the blue sphere). In this situation you must act immediately to provide <u>C</u>hest <u>C</u>ompressions. After <u>C</u>hest <u>C</u>ompressions you open the patient's <u>A</u>irway and then <u>B</u>reathe for the patient (<u>CAB</u>). As defined earlier, this is how CPR is administered.

Once you are finished providing rescue breaths for the patient, you return to Chest Compressions and begin again. You continue CPR in a continuous cycle of chest compressions, re-opening the airway and breathe for the patient. We call this the *Cycle of Care*.

If you find a patient who is breathing normally, then he does not need CPR. You SKIP all the steps in the blue sphere – the <u>CAB</u> portion of the memory word. In this situation you move along the *Cycle of Care* to the S portion of CAB<u>S</u> and treat the patient for <u>S</u>erious bleeding, <u>S</u>hock and <u>S</u>pinal injury.

Notice that if you are performing CPR on a patient who is not breathing normally you continue with <u>C</u>hest <u>C</u>ompressions, opening the <u>A</u>irway and providing rescue <u>B</u>reaths – <u>CAB</u>. You do not attempt to treat the patient for serious bleeding, shock and spinal injury. CPR takes priority over all other concerns.

Continually Move Through The *Cycle of Care*

Regardless of a patient's situation upon your arrival, you begin a primary assessment using the memory word AB-CABS to help you remember how to begin and what steps to follow. Remember the word AB-CABS and think of the *Cycle of Care* graphic.

The phrase, "Continually move through the *Cycle of Care*" helps you maintain appropriate primary care sequencing. In a continual *Cycle of Care* you deliver CPR, remembering the CAB portion of the memory word. You do this until professional help (ambulance or Emergency Medical Services) arrives or an Automated External Defibrillator (AED) is located and brought to the patient. More on AED's in the next topic.

Let's apply the priorities indicated by the *Cycle of Care* to two different situations.

Cycle of Care: AB-CABS™

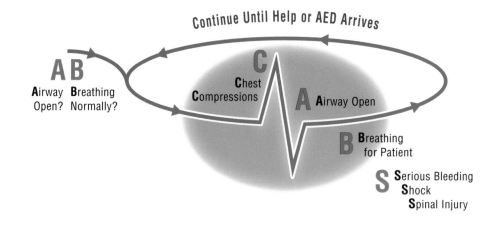

Continue Until Help or AED Arrives

A B
Airway Breathing
Open? Normally?

C Chest Compressions

A Airway Open

B Breathing for Patient

S Serious Bleeding
Shock
Spinal Injury

Situation One

Choose the correct sequence of care by numbering the actions (1 to 8) below based on this scenario:

You are alone and find a patient lying in his yard. He is unresponsive and not breathing normally. He has fallen on a sharp gardening tool and it has impaled his leg. His leg is bleeding. For this patient, what is the sequence of emergency care? You should:

_____ Assess the scene for unknown dangers to yourself and the patient and apply barriers
_____ Alert EMS
_____ Breathe for the patient - give rescue breaths
_____ Continue with CPR until help or an AED arrives
_____ Provide patient with chest compressions
_____ Apply direct pressure to the bleeding leg
_____ Check for an open airway and normal breathing
_____ Open the patient's airway

Correct Sequence: 1) Assess the scene for unknown dangers to yourself and the patient and apply barriers, 2) Check for an open airway and normal breathing, 3) Alert EMS, 4) Provide patient with chest compressions, 5) Open the patient's airway, 6) Breathe for the patient - give rescue breaths, 7) Continue CPR until help or an AED arrives, 8) Apply direct pressure to the bleeding leg.

NOTE – You would only attend to the bleeding leg if the patient became responsive and was breathing normally. Otherwise, you would continue CPR until relieved by EMS.

Situation Two

Choose the correct sequence of care by numbering the actions (1-5) below based on this scenario:

A painter falls from a tall ladder onto cement. When you find him he is moaning and talking, but obviously hurt. For this patient, what is the proper sequence of emergency care?

_____ Look for and treat suspected bleeding, shock and/or spinal injury

_____ Alert EMS

_____ Continually move through the *Cycle of Care* until EMS arrives

_____ Assess the scene for unknown dangers to yourself and the patient

_____ Check for an open airway and normal breathing

Correct Sequence: 1) Assess the scene for unknown dangers to yourself and the patient, 2) Check for an open airway and normal breathing, 3) Alert EMS, 4) Look for and treat suspected bleeding, shock and/or spinal injury, 5) Continually move through the *Cycle of Care* until EMS arrives.

In this situation the patient is responsive and talking. If a patient talks and moans, then he has an open airway and is breathing. He does not need CPR, so you skip the **CAB** portion of the *Cycle of Care*. You would provide care for possible **S**erious bleeding, **S**hock and/or **S**pinal injury.

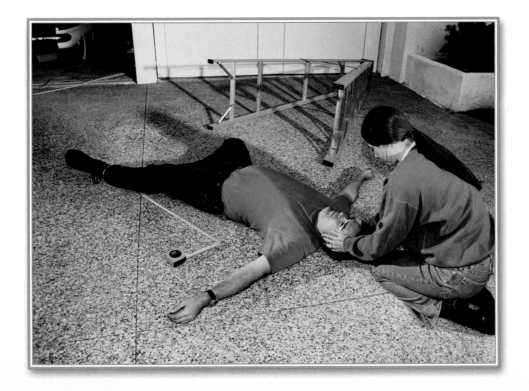

Importance of an AED and Defibrillation

A heartbeat is triggered by electrical impulses. When these natural electrical impulses malfunction, the heart begins to beat erratically. This is called *ventricular fibrillation*. Fibrillation means to twitch.

Ventricular fibrillation causes sudden heart attacks. To stop the heart from twitching erratically, an Automated External Defibrillator (AED) is used to deliver an electrical shock, disrupting this abnormal twitching. The momentary disruption can allow the heart's normal heartbeat to return.

Administering an electrical shock from an AED is called *defibrillation*. Since ventricular fibrillation is one of the most common life-threatening heart-related emergencies, prompt defibrillation is vital to the *Chain of Survival*.

Study Questions

♦ What is defibrillation and why is it important to a patient whose heart has stopped?

♦ When a patient's heart is beating erratically or quivering (ventricular fibrillation), how can it be restored to a normal heart rhythm?

♦ What is an Automated External Defibrillator (AED)?

How AEDs Work

An AED is a portable machine that automatically delivers a shock to a patient who is not breathing normally and whose heart has stopped beating or is beating irregularly.

AEDs connect to a patient via two chest pads. When the AED is turned on, its computer analyzes the patient's need for a shock. If the AED detects a shockable heart rhythm, the machine will indicate that a shock is advised. Depending on the type of AED, either the Emergency Responder will activate the shock or the machine does so automatically. You may have an orientation to an AED as an optional skill in the Emergency First Response Primary Care (CPR) course.

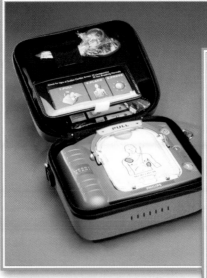

An AED is an easy-to-use, portable machine that automatically delivers a shock to a patient who is not breathing and has no heartbeat.

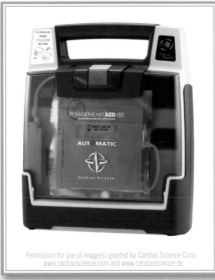

Permission for use of image(s) granted by Cardiac Science Corp.. www.cardiacscience.com and www.cardiacscience.de

AED's vary by manufacturer.

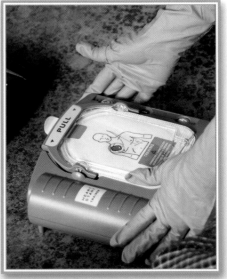

Properly operating an AED is simple with a little training.

Serious Bleeding, Shock and Spinal Injury

If a patient's **A**irway is open and he's **B**reathing normally (**AB**), then there is no need to provide chest compressions, make sure his airway is open or breathe for the patient. In other words, there is no need to act on the "CAB" portion of the *Cycle of Care*.

Since you can skip the **CAB** portion of the *Cycle of Care*, you next check the patient for **S**erious bleeding, **S**hock, and **S**pinal injuries. These comprise the "S" in the word "CAB**S**," and each needs to be managed by Emergency Responders to effectively help a patient. Let's look at each separately.

Cycle of Care: AB-CABS™

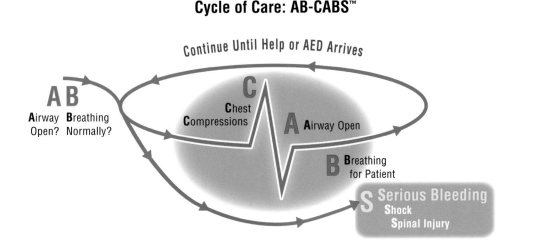

Serious Bleeding

Experience tells you that when the skin and underlying tissue is cut, scraped or punctured, there's going to be blood. How much blood flows from the wound and how quickly it leaves the body is what determines whether it's a minor problem or serious bleeding. The human body contains about six litres/quarts of blood. Rapid loss of just one litre/quart is dangerous and can lead to death. Because serious bleeding is life-threatening, you, as an Emergency Responder, need to be able to recognize and manage this during a primary assessment. **S**erious bleeding is the first S in AB-CAB**S** *Cycle of Care*.

In general, there are three types of bleeding. In an emergency, it's not critical for you to diagnose the exact type of bleeding. However, by knowing the differences, you'll be better able to judge how serious the wound is and how best to manage it. During skill development, you'll learn how to control bleeding.

Study Questions

- What are the three types of bleeding and how is each identified?

- What is shock, what can cause it, and what are the nine indications of shock?

- What does the spinal cord do in the human body and why is it important to protect the spinal cord during primary care.

- What eight indications might signal the need for spinal injury management

- In what nine circumstances should you always suspect a spinal injury?

- What are the five situations when you might want to move an injured or ill person?

Arterial Bleeding – Arterial bleeding can be recognized when bright red blood spurts from a wound in rhythm with the heartbeat. This is the most serious type of bleeding since blood loss occurs very quickly. If a major artery is cut, death can occur within a minute.

Venous Bleeding– Venous bleeding can be recognized when dark red blood steadily flows from the wound without rhythmic spurts. This bleeding can also be life-threatening and must be controlled as quickly as possible.

Capillary Bleeding – Capillary bleeding can be recognized when blood slowly oozes from the wound. Capillary bleeding may stop on it's own or is typically easy to handle with direct pressure.

Any time a patient has serious bleeding, use barriers, activate EMS immediately, and quickly render care to prevent excessive blood loss. During the Skill Development session, you will learn how to control bleeding and provide emergency care.

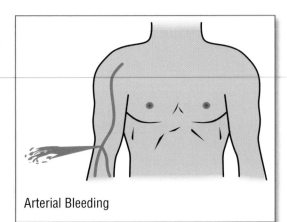

Arterial Bleeding

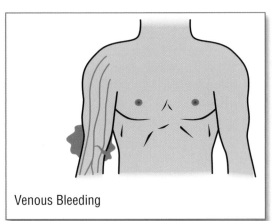

Venous Bleeding

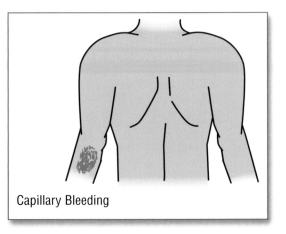

Capillary Bleeding

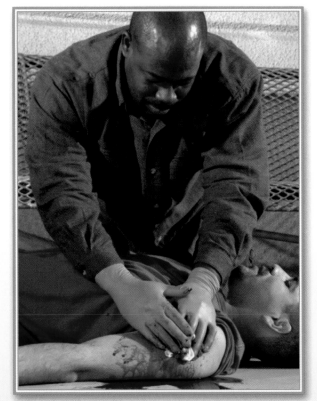

Experience tells you that when the skin and underlying tissue is cut, scraped or punctured, there's going to be blood.

Shock

Any injury or illness, serious or minor, which stresses the body, may result in shock. In reaction to a medical condition, the body pools blood into one or more vital organs. This reduces normal blood flow to other body tissues depriving cells of oxygen. During shock, the body begins to shut down. Shock is a life-threatening condition that is easier to prevent from getting worse than it is to treat after it becomes severe. **S**hock management is the second S in AB-CAB**S** *Cycle of Care.*

During primary assessment and care, you take the first steps to managing shock by dealing with other life-threatening conditions. Checking that a patient is breathing, has adequate circulation and is not bleeding profusely helps the patient's body maintain normal blood flow. You render additional care by keeping the patient still and maintaining the patient's body temperature. You may elevate the patient's legs if it won't aggravate another injury. Continuing to monitor the *Cycle of Care* until EMS arrives also contributes to shock management. The nine indications of shock are:

Manage shock by keeping the patient still and maintaining the patient's body temperature.

- Rapid, weak pulse
- Pale or bluish tissue color
- Moist, clammy skin – possibly with shivering
- Mental confusion, anxiety, restlessness or irritability
- Altered consciousness
- Nausea and perhaps vomiting
- Thirst
- Lackluster eyes, dazed look
- Shallow, but rapid, labored breathing

Even if you don't recognize any of these signs and symptoms in a patient, continue to manage for shock when you provide emergency care to an injured or ill patient. It's better to prevent shock than to let it complicate a patient's condition.

You may also elevate the patient's legs to manage shock.

During the Skill Development session, you will learn how to manage shock and provide emergency care.

Cycle of Care: AB-CABS™

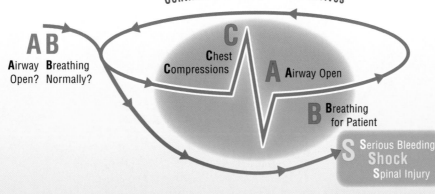

Continue Until Help or AED Arrives

A **B**
Airway **B**reathing
Open? Normally?

C
Chest
Compressions

A **A**irway Open

B **B**reathing
for Patient

S **S**erious Bleeding
Shock
Spinal Injury

Spinal Injury

The spinal cord connects the brain with the rest of the body and organs. Nerve impulses, or messages between the brain and the body, travel through the spinal cord. An intact, functioning spinal cord is essential for life.

Vertebrae are rings of bones surrounding the spinal cord and run from the neck to the lower back. These bones make up the backbone, or spinal column.

A spinal cord injury may result in permanent paralysis or death. The higher up in the spinal column the injury, the more likely it will cause a serious disability. This is why it's so important to guard the head, neck and spine when attending to an injured patient.

Important: **Never move a patient unless absolutely necessary.**

A patient with a severe spinal injury will likely be unable to move. However, a less severe spinal injury will not necessarily keep a patient down. Accident victims often try to get up and move away from the scene. Because an injured spinal cord is fragile, allowing a patient to walk around could turn a minor injury into a permanent disability.

If you suspect a neck or spinal cord injury, keep the patient still and support the head to minimize movement. If you must open the patient's airway, use the chin lift method – do not tilt or move the patient's head. If CPR is necessary and you must position the patient flat on the back, turn the patient as a unit – avoid twisting or jarring the spine.

If you didn't see the injury occur or the circumstances surrounding an injury are not clear, look for these indications that may signal the need for spinal injury management:

1. Change of consciousness – like fainting
2. Difficulty breathing
3. Vision problems
4. Inability to move a body part
5. Headache
6. Vomiting
7. Loss of balance
8. Tingling or numbness in hands, fingers and feet and/or toes
9. Pain in back of neck area

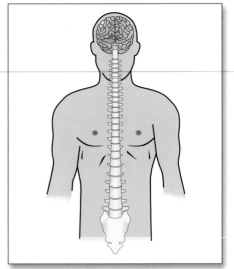

The spinal cord is surrounded by vertebrae that protect it. A serious blow, fall or jolt could cause a break and damage the cord.

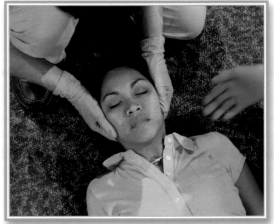

If you suspect a neck or spinal cord injury, keep the patient still and support the head to minimize movement.

Cycle of Care: AB-CABS™

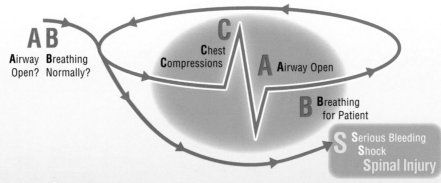

Continue Until Help or AED Arrives

Airway Open? **B**reathing Normally?

Chest Compressions

Airway Open

Breathing for Patient

Serious Bleeding
Shock
Spinal Injury

These are common indications of a back or neck injury, however none may be present even though the patient has an injury. So, regardless of whether these indications are present or not, if you think a person has an injured neck or back, treat it as such.

Spinal injuries generally result from falls or other blows associated with accidents. There may be other incidents that injure the spine, but you should always suspect a spinal injury in these circumstances:

1. Traffic/car accident
2. Being thrown from a motorized vehicle
3. Falling from a height greater than patient's own height
4. A penetration wound, such as a gunshot
5. Severe blow to the head, neck or back
6. Swimming pool, head-first dive accident
7. Lightning strike
8. Serious impact injury
9. Patient complains of pain in neck or back

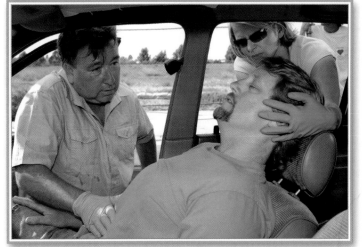

Spinal injuries generally result from falls or other blows associated with accidents.

If You Must Move a Patient

As just discussed, you should move an injured or ill person only if it's absolutely necessary. This includes circumstances of clear and direct danger to the patient's life, or if emergency care is impossible due to a patient's location or position. Situations in which you may need to move a patient to give emergency care include:

• Patient is in water
• Patient is near a burning object or structure that may explode
• Patient is under an unstable structure that may collapse
• Patient is on an unstable slope
• Patient is on a roadway and you can't effectively direct traffic away from patient's location

Only move a patient when the location is hazardous or prevents you from providing care.

Many other situations may apply. You may discuss these with your instructor during skill development while you learn and practice the steps for scene assessment. By taking a moment to assess an accident scene, you help protect yourself from life-threatening hazards and prevent the patient from suffering further harm. During skill development, you'll also practice turning a patient while protecting the neck and spine. This technique for moving a patient is called the *log roll*. You'll learn to roll a patient by yourself and with the assistance of another Emergency Responder.

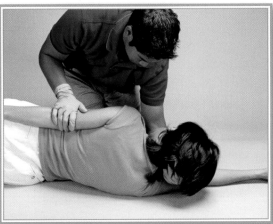

During skill development, you'll also practice turning a patient while protecting the neck and spine.

Primary Care Knowledge Review

Name: _____ Date: _____

1. When someone needs emergency care, time is critical because: *(Check all that apply.)*
   - _____ a. It becomes more difficult to administer first aid.
   - _____ b. The chances of successful resuscitation diminish with time.
   - ✓ c. When a person has no heartbeat and is not breathing, irreversible brain damage can occur within minutes.

2. Give three reasons why you should assist someone who needs emergency care:
   - a. _____
   - b. _____
   - c. _____

3. Of the six reasons causing people to hesitate when providing emergency care to a patient, name three:
   - a. _____
   - b. _____
   - c. _____

4. Good Samaritan laws are enacted to encourage people to come to the aid of others. Generally, they protect individuals who voluntarily offer assistance to those in need. _____ True _____ False

5. To be protected by Good Samaritan laws you should: *(Check all that apply.)*
   - _____ a. Only provide care that is within the scope of your training as an Emergency Responder.
   - _____ b. Ask for permission to help
   - _____ c. Act in good faith.
   - _____ d. Do not be reckless or negligent.
   - _____ e. Avoid helping an injured or ill person when others are around.
   - _____ f. Act as a prudent person would.
   - _____ g. Do not abandon the patient once you begin care. The exception to this is if you must do so to protect yourself from imminent danger.

6. Name the Chain of Survival's four links in the spaces below.

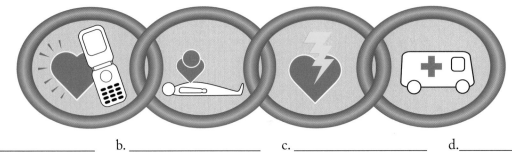

   a. _____ b. _____ c. _____ d._____

7. From the introductory statements below, which one would you select when asking permission to help a patient?
   - _____ a. I'm a doctor. May I help you?
   - ✓ b. Hello? My name is _____MAC_____, I'm an Emergency Responder. May I help you?
   - _____ c. Are you hurt? Where?

8. After establishing patient unresponsiveness and identifying that he is not breathing normally, you should:
   _____
   _____
   _____

9. How do you activate the Emergency Medical Service in your area? Phone number: _____

10. Why should you never fear harming a patient when performing CPR on an individual who is unresponsive and is not breathing normally?
    _____
    _____
    _____

11. When not used or practiced, your primary care skills will deteriorate over time. It's a good idea to take a Refresher course at least every 12 to 24 months to keep your skills current. _____ True _____ False

12. As an Emergency Responder what general rule may help you avoid infection by bloodborne pathogens?
    _____✓___ a. Always place a barrier between you and any moist or wet substance originating from a patient.
    _____ b. Ask the patient not to cough when you are giving him emergency care.
    _____ c. Have the patient bandage his own bleeding wounds whenever possible.

13. List six common signs and symptoms of a stroke:
    1. _____   4. _____
    2. _____   5. _____
    3. _____   6. _____

14. Primary Assessment means:
    _____ a. Checking a patient's breathing.
    _____ b. Providing direct pressure on a bleeding wound.
    _____ c. An Emergency Responder's first evaluation of an injured or ill person.

15. CPR stands for: _____ Cardio Pulmonary resustition. _____

16. Fill in the missing meaning for each letter on the *Cycle of Care* graphic.
    C = _____
    A = _____
    B = _____
    S = _____

Cycle of Care: AB-CABS™

Continue Until Help or AED Arrives

A B
Airway Breathing
Open? Normally?

C

A

B

S Shock
Spinal Injury

17. Why is defibrillation important to a patient with cardiac arrest?
    ___✗___ a. Defibrillation disrupts the abnormal twitching of a heart, restoring a normal heartbeat.
    _____ b. Defibrillation causes the heart to beat erratically.
    _____ c. It keeps the patient from having to go to the hospital after CPR has been administered.

18. Match the type of bleeding listed below with the description of how each is identified.
    (Draw a line from the description to the type of bleeding.)
    a. Arterial Bleeding   a Dark red blood, steadily flowing from a wound without rhythmic spurts.
    b. Venous Bleeding   c Blood slowly oozing from the wound.
    c. Capillary Bleeding   b Bright red blood that spurts from a wound in rhythm with the heartbeat.

19. What are indications of shock. *(Check all that apply.)*
    ___✓___ a. Pale or bluish tissue color
    ___✓___ b. Altered consciousness
    ___✓___ c. Lackluster eyes, dazed look
    _____ d. Thirst
    ___✓___ e. Rapid, weak pulse
    _____ f. Elbow pain
    ___✓___ g. Mental confusion, anxiety, restlessness or irritability
    ___✓___ h. Nausea and perhaps vomiting
    ___✓___ i. Moist, clammy skin, perhaps with shivering
    ___✓___ j. Shallow, but rapid and labored breathing
    _____ k. Earache

20. In what circumstances should you always suspect a spinal injury? *(Check all that apply.)*
    _____ a. Lightning strike
    _____ b. A penetration wound, such as a gunshot
    ___✓___ c. Falling from a height greater than victim's own height
    ___✓___ d. Traffic or car accident
    ___✓___ e. Being thrown from a motorized vehicle
    ___✓___ f. Swimming pool, head-first dive accident

Secondary Care **First Aid**

Introduction

Every day people have mishaps or get sick. Some may be involved in bad accidents or suffer from serious illness, yet remain conscious and responsive. Their conditions may not be immediately life-threatening, yet they still need medical care.

Emergency First Response Secondary Care (First Aid) teaches you to assist injured or ill patients by offering first aid and support while waiting for Emergency Medical Service (EMS) personnel. The course prepares you to render emergency care for common medical problems that are not immediately life-threatening.

As you learned in your Emergency First Response Primary Care (or other CPR) course, any time you approach a patient to provide emergency care, regardless of the injury or illness, you perform a primary assessment and monitor the patient using the *Cycle of Care*. During this course, you'll review the *Cycle of Care* – assuring there is no imminent threat to the patient's life – then practice providing secondary care that reassures the patient, eases pain and reduces the risk of further harm.

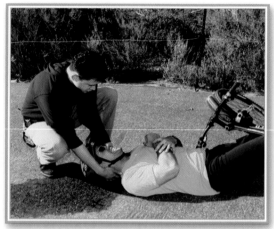

You provide secondary care to an ill or injured patient who is responsive.

If EMS is nearby, you may never need to use the secondary care skills in this course. However, if EMS is unavailable or delayed or there is time and distance between the patient and professional medical care, you may need to use the secondary care skills learned in this course to render first aid.

Four Skills of Emergency First Response® Secondary Care

▶ Injury Assessment

▶ Illness Assessment

▶ Bandaging

▶ Splinting for Dislocations and Fractures

Secondary Care Definitions and Background Information

Secondary means *second in a series or sequence.* An assessment is an *evaluation* or *appraisal.* Secondary assessment is your second evaluation of an injured or ill person.

Once a patient is stabilized during primary care, you attend to the next level of emergency care – *secondary care.* This is the care you provide to a patient with injuries or illnesses that are not immediately life-threatening.

During skill development, you'll practice injury assessment that helps you determine the location and extent of all the patient's injuries. You'll also learn the steps for illness assessment that help you identify and report medical problems that affect a patient's health and may aid in treatment. Bandaging wounds, sprains and strains along with splinting dislocations and fractures round out the skills you need to provide secondary care.

The Difference Between Injury and Illness

Throughout this manual, you've read the words injury and illness. When discussing secondary care, it's important to understand exactly what these terms mean.

An injury is defined as *physical harm to the body*.

Examples include:

▶ Cuts, scrapes and bruises

▶ Chest wounds

▶ Head, eye and dental wounds

▶ Burns

▶ Dislocations and fractures

▶ Temperature-related problems – hypothermia, frostbite, heat exhaustion and heat stroke

▶ Electrical injuries

An illness is an *unhealthy condition of the body*. Illnesses may be caused by preexisting conditions such as allergies, heart disease or diabetes. They may also occur due to external factors such as breathing toxic fumes or ingesting poison. Generally, illnesses are determined by looking for clues or signs that the patient's body is stressed and also by listening to the patient describe symptoms.

Study Questions

◆ What is a Secondary Assessment and Secondary Care?

◆ What is the difference between injury and illness?

◆ What is Assessment First Aid?

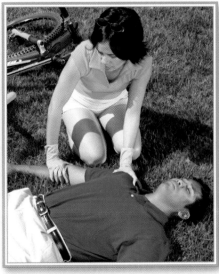

Injury Assessment

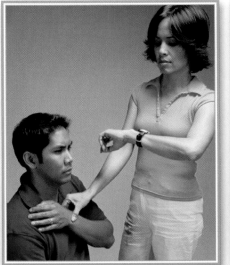

Illness Assessment

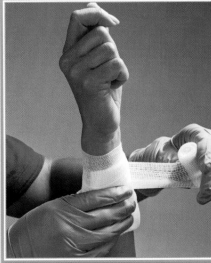

Bandaging

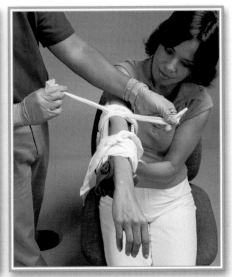

Splinting for Dislocation and Fracture

Signs and Symptoms

▶ A sign is something you can *see, hear* or *feel.*

▶ For an injury assessment you look for signs such as wounds, bleeding, discolorations, or deformities. You also listen for unusual breathing sounds and feel for swelling or hardness, tissue softness or unusual masses.

▶ For an illness assessment you look for changes in skin color, breathing rate or patient awareness along with shivering or seizures. You listen for breathing difficulty and you feel the patient's skin temperature and pulse.

▶ A symptom is something the *patient tells* you is wrong.

▶ For both injury and illness assessments, the patient may complain of nausea, thirst, dizziness, numbness or pain.

You look, listen and feel for signs.

A symptom is something the *patient tells* you is wrong.

Medical Alert Tags

In a medical emergency, information is critical. People with serious medical conditions or severe allergies may wear medical alert tags to provide instant information to Emergency Responders. Usually worn as necklaces, bracelets or other jewelry, these tags may list the patient's medical problem, medications, allergies and physician, hospital or relative contact numbers.

When a patient is unresponsive or is having difficulty communicating, check for a medical alert tag. It can provide you with the information you need to provide proper care.

What is Normal?

It's difficult to determine if an ill patient's signs are abnormal if you don't know what is "normal." The fact is that what is normal for one patient may be completely abnormal for another. There are "normal" ranges for breathing rate, pulse and skin temperature. However, a patient could be outside the average and still be within a personal "normal" range. This is why it's important when giving information to EMS personnel to avoid using the word *normal* and simply provide measured rates per minute and use other descriptive terminology.

Here are the average ranges that may help guide your assessment:

▶ The average breathing rate for adults is between 12 and 20 breaths per minute. A patient who takes less than 8 breaths per minute, or more than 24 breaths per minute, probably needs immediate medical care.

▶ The average pulse rate for adults is between 60-80 beats per minute.

▶ Average skin temperature is warm and skin should feel dry to the touch.

Assessment First Aid

Assessment first aid is the *treatment of conditions that are not immediately life-threatening,* uncovered during either an illness assessment or an injury assessment. For example, applying a bandage to a wound or wrapping a shivering patient in a warm blanket is assessment first aid.

Although the emphasis of the Emergency First Response Secondary Care (First Aid) course is on rendering emergency care until EMS arrives, you'll find that you may also use your skills to handle common minor medical problems. Cleaning and dressing a child's scraped knee is assessment first aid. Placing a cool compress on a family member's head to relieve flu symptoms is also assessment first aid.

In every situation that involves injury and illness, you'll follow the sequence and steps that you learn and practice in this course. For emergency care and first aid information that is more specific, for example – what to do for snakebite, use the reference section of your *Emergency First Response Participant Manual.*

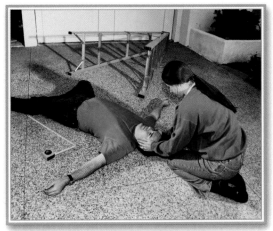

Assessment first aid is the treatment of conditions that are not immediately life-threatening.

Secondary Care **Knowledge Review**

Name: _____ Date: _____

1. Regardless of a patient's injury or illness, you perform a _____ assessment and monitor the patient's
    _____ . *(Place the correct letter in the blank.)*

    _____   a.   secondary; line of life

    _____   b.   primary; *Cycle of Care*

2. Once a patient is stabilized during primary care, you attend to the next level of emergency care - _____ .

    _____   a.   injury care

    _____   b.   secondary care

3. An injury is defined as _____.

4. An illness is defined as _____.

5. A symptom is: *(Place a check by your response.)*

    _____   a.   something the patient tells you is wrong

    _____   b.   something you can see, hear or feel

6. Assessment first aid is the treatment of conditions that are not immediately _____ .

Section TWO

Skills WORKBOOK

Contents

Primary Care (CPR)

Secondary Care (First Aid)

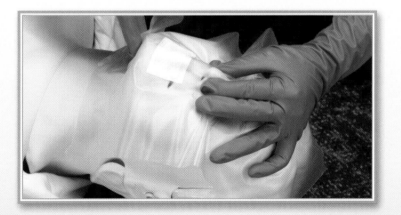

Primary Care CPR

Primary Care Skill 1
Scene Assessment

Cycle of Care: AB-CABS™

Continue Until Help or AED Arrives

C Chest Compressions

A Airway Open

B Breathing for Patient

S Serious Bleeding
Shock
Spinal Injury

AB

A Airway Open?

B Breathing Normally?

Assess Scene
Apply Barriers
Airway Open?

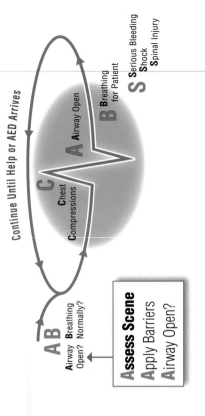

Your Goal

Demonstrate the procedures for assessing an emergency scene for safety.

How It's Done

1 STOP – Assess Scene

▲ Ask yourself – What caused the injury?

▲ Are there any hazards? Look for potential hazards such as leaking gas, chemicals, radiation, downed electrical lines, fire, firearms, the possibility of explosion, oxygen depletion, etc.

▲ Can you make a safe approach? Consider how to make a safe approach. Be alert for possible dangers, such as oncoming traffic. Do you need to turn off a car's engine?

▲ Apply barriers as appropriate and if available.

2 THINK – Formulate Safe Action Plan

▲ Can you remain safe while helping? Remember that your safety must be the first priority. Know your limitations.

▲ What emergency care may be needed?

▲ How can you activate local EMS?

▲ Think about your training and relax.

3 ACT – Begin Providing Care

▲ Follow the emergency care guidelines you will learn in upcoming skills.

▲ Continue to consider your safety as you provide care.

TRY IT In your practice group, work through the scene assessment steps for the scenarios on the next page. Use steps 1-3 – STOP, THINK and ACT – to assess the scene and form an action plan.

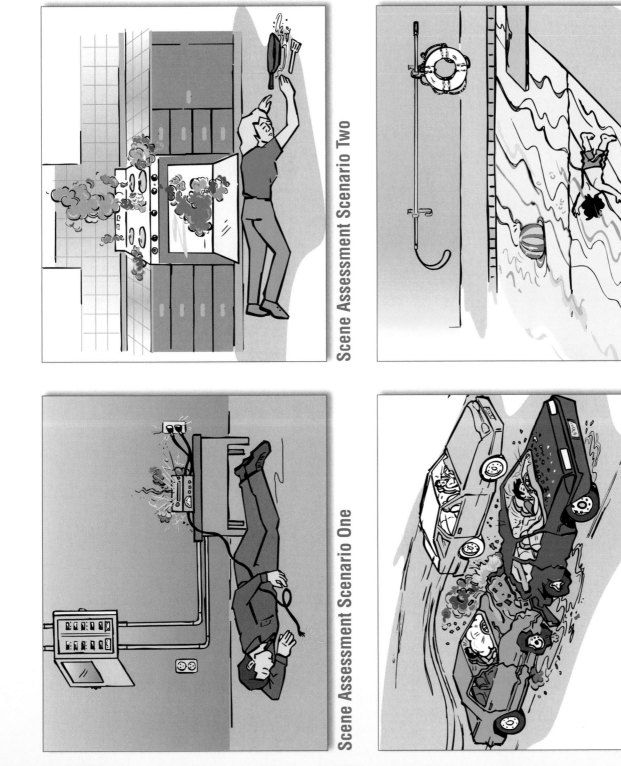

Scene Assessment Scenario Two

Scene Assessment Scenario Four

Scene Assessment Scenario One

Scene Assessment Scenario Three

Primary Care Skill 2
Barrier Use

Your Goal

Demonstrate procedures for donning, removing and disposing of gloves. This includes removing gloves without snapping or tearing them. Also, properly position a ventilation barrier on a mannequin.

How It's Done

Gloves On

1 Quickly put on gloves. Pull them on carefully to avoid tearing. Consider removing sharp rings on fingers.

Cycle of Care: **AB-CABS**™

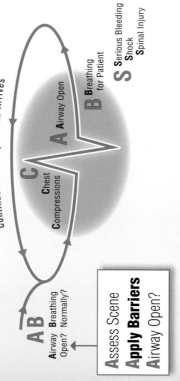

Assess Scene
Apply Barriers
Airway Open?

A B
Airway Breathing
Open? Normally?

Continue Until Help or AED Arrives

C Chest
Compressions

A Airway Open

B Breathing
for Patient

S Serious Bleeding
Shock
Spinal Injury

Key Points

◆ Remember to STOP, THINK and then ACT.

◆ Barriers include gloves, ventilation barriers, eye shields and face masks.

◆ IMPORTANT: Do NOT delay emergency patient care if barriers are not available. Research has shown that the chance of disease transmission is very rare when providing CPR.

◆ If gloves and ventilation barriers are immediately available, use them during CPR to protect yourself and the patient from possible disease transmission.

◆ If available, also use eye shields and face masks when patients have serious bleeding.

◆ Prior to and after all skill practice, wash your hands. After providing actual emergency care, make sure you wash your hands.

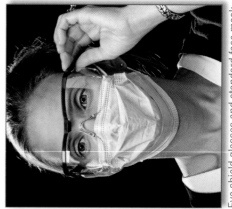

Eye shield glasses and standard face mask.

Consider using eye shields and face masks when necessary, especially when a patient has serious bleeding. This Emergency Responder is using a barrier that is both a face mask and a plastic eye shield in one.

Step Two

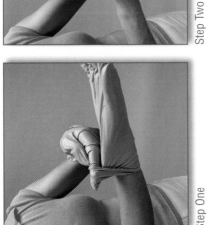
Step One

Step Four

Step Three

Ventilation Barriers and Disposal

Gloves Off

1 Gloves can become contaminated during use – remove them carefully. To remove the first soiled glove, carefully pinch the outside portion of the glove at wrist. Avoid contact with the outside of the glove. Be careful not to snap or tear the glove during removal. Step one.

2 Gently roll glove off so that the outside portion is turned inside. Hold the removed glove with the gloved hand. Step two.

3 To remove the second glove, place the ungloved hand under the glove at the wrist, next to the skin, and roll off in the same manner. Roll the second glove off and around the first removed glove. Step three.

4 After removing both gloves, place them in biohazard bag for disposal. Step four.

Ventilation Barriers

1 Place ventilation barrier over patient's mouth and/or nose. See photos for placement of different types and hand positions.

2 Position ventilation barrier to allow rescue breaths.

3 Place used, disposable ventilation barrier in biohazard bag. Clean and disinfect non-disposable ventilation barrier after use.

TRY IT

In your practice group, carefully put on and take off your gloves. Be careful not to tear or snap them as fluids may disperse inappropriately. Also, practice placing ventilation barriers on a mannequin, as directed by your instructor.

Primary Care Skill 3
Primary Assessment – Airway Open? Breathing Normally?

Your Goals

Demonstrate how to:

▲ Perform a patient responsiveness check by giving the Responder Statement and tapping the patient's collarbone.

▲ Check for an open airway using one of two methods: head tilt-chin lift or pistol grip lift.

▲ Check for normal breathing.

▲ Perform a Primary Assessment on a conscious and responsive patient.

▲ Perform a Primary Assessment on an unresponsive and unconscious patient.

▲ Place an unresponsive, breathing patient in the recovery position.

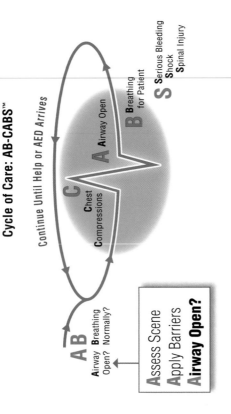

Cycle of Care: AB-CABS™

Continue Until Help or AED Arrives

C Chest Compressions

A Airway Open

B Breathing for Patient

S Serious Bleeding, Shock, Spinal Injury

A Airway Open? **B** Breathing Normally?

Assess Scene
Apply Barriers
Airway Open?

Key Points

◆ Use the *Cycle of Care* graphic and the memory word AB-CABS to help you conduct a Primary Assessment.

◆ Deliver the Responder Statement and tap collarbone to check for patient responsiveness.

◆ Check for normal breathing. If the patient is not breathing or is only gasping, then he needs CPR.

◆ Avoid delaying emergency care by taking the time to locate and put on barriers.

◆ If an unresponsive patient is obviously breathing normally, use the *Cycle of Care* to continually monitor his medical status. Check for Serious bleeding, Shock or Spinal injury. Next, put the patient in the recovery position.

◆ The recovery position relieves pressure on the patient's chest, allowing the patient to breathe more easily. It also ensures the airway remains open and unobstructed while at the same time decreasing the risk of something blocking his airway, and allowing fluids to drain should he vomit.

Checking for Normal Breathing

Check Responsiveness

Keep Patient Still

Manage Possible Spinal Injury

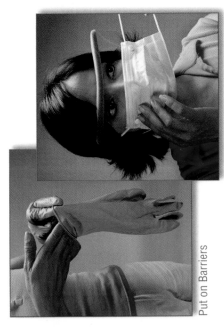

Alert EMS

Manage Shock

Put on Barriers

How It's Done

For a responsive patient

1 Assess the scene for dangers. Check the patient for responsiveness by giving the Responder Statement: *Hello? My Name is _____ . I'm an Emergency Responder. May I help you?* If no response to your statement, then tap the patient on collarbone and ask, *Are you okay? Are you okay?* The collarbone is sensitive and tapping it will reveal a level of responsiveness.

2 A verbal response from the patient means that he is responsive, confirms he has an open airway, is breathing normally and has a heartbeat. Therefore, CPR is not needed – do not begin chest compressions. Specifically, there is NO need to act on the CAB portion of the memory word – Chest Compressions, opening the Airway or Breathing for the patient.

3 Alert EMS if appropriate. The EMS phone number for this local area is:
_____

4 Keep the patient still – do not move the patient (unless you or the patient's safety is compromised).

5 If you have not done so already, put on barriers if immediately at hand. However, do not delay emergency care if barriers are absent.

6 Continue your Primary Assessment with the "S" portion of the memory word CABS – Serious bleeding, Shock and Spinal injury management. (You'll learn how to manage these emergency care concerns later.)

7 Continue with the *Cycle of Care* to monitor a patient's medical status. The patient could lapse into unresponsiveness and stop breathing normally.

Step Two

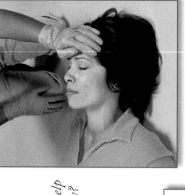

Step One

Step Three

Unresponsive – Call for Help and Perform CPR

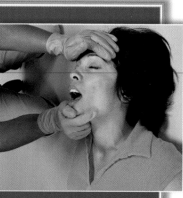

Pistol Grip Lift

For an unresponsive patient

1 Assess the scene for safety. Check the patient for responsiveness by giving the Responder Statement: *Hello? My Name is _____. I'm an Emergency Responder. May I help you?* If no response to your statement, then tap the patient on collarbone and ask, *Are you okay? Are you okay?* The collarbone is sensitive and tapping it will reveal a level of responsiveness.

2 Quickly check for an open Airway and normal Breathing. If you are unsure if the patient's airway is open or if he is breathing normally:

▲ Quickly open his airway using the head tilt-chin lift. Place your hand on his forehead and gently tilt his head back. Step one. With your fingertips under the point of his chin, lift the chin to open the airway. Step two.

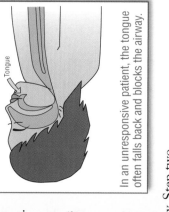

Tongue

In an unresponsive patient, the tongue often falls back and blocks the airway.

Use the head tilt-chin lift to open a blocked airway.

▲ Check for normal breathing. Look for chest movement and listen for breathing sounds. Feel for expired air on your cheek. Step three.

▲ This check for normal breathing must be accomplished quickly. If the patient is not breathing normally, he needs CPR immediately.

3 If the patient is not responsive or breathing normally, ask a bystander to call EMS and secure an AED if possible. If you are alone, use your mobile phone to call EMS. If you do not have a mobile phone, leave the patient to call EMS if no other option exists. This is the *Call First* approach to emergency care. You *Call First* to activate Emergency Medical Services, then you provide assistance.

Pistol Grip Lift – Alternative to Head Tilt-Chin Lift

◆ With your thumb and index finger, point it like a pretend handgun.

◆ Place your thumb and index finger together, as if you "fired" the gun.

◆ Place your thumb and index finger along the patient's jaw line. Your thumb is just below the patient's lip and your index finger is positioned across the patient's chin.

◆ Use your thumb, index finger and middle fingers to open the patient's lips and mouth. Keep other fingers off the soft tissue of the neck.

◆ Place your other hand on the patient's forehead.

◆ Gently lift the patient's jaw with your middle finger and tilt head back.

Step One

Step Two

Step Three

Step Four

Recovery Position

For an unresponsive patient *(continued)*

4 Put on barriers if immediately at hand. Do not delay emergency care if barriers are absent.

5 If the patient is unresponsive and NOT BREATHING NORMALLY, immediately begin giving CPR. (You will learn CPR in the next skill. DO NOT PRACTICE CPR ON ANOTHER PARTICIPANT.)

6 If the patient is unresponsive BUT IS BREATHING NORMALLY, continue your Primary Assessment with the "S" portion of the memory word CABS – check for Serious bleeding, Shock and Spinal injury. (You learn how to manage these emergency care concerns later.)

7 If no serious bleeding, shock or spinal injury is found or suspected, place the unresponsive, breathing patient in the recovery position:

▲ Kneel at the patient's side and place the arm nearest you out at a right angle to the patient's body with the elbow bent and the palm upward. Step one.

▲ Bring the far arm across the chest and hold the back of the hand against the patient's cheek nearest you. Step two.

▲ With your other hand, grasp the far leg just above the knee and pull it up, keeping the foot on the ground. Step three.

▲ Now, gently pull the patient towards you, putting the patient on his side. Step four. Once on his side, place the patient's lower hand near or under the neck for stabilization. If need be, gently pull back on the patient's head to assure an open airway.

8 If the patient has to be kept in the recovery position for more than 30 minutes, consider turning the patient to the opposite side to relieve the pressure on the lower arm.

TRY IT

In your practice group perform a Primary Assessment on a responsive patient and also on an unresponsive patient who is not breathing normally. One person is the guide, reading the steps; one is the patient, while the other is the Emergency Responder. Everyone should have the chance to act as the Emergency Responder. Also, for an unresponsive, normal breathing patient, practice putting the patient in the recovery position. Alter circumstances as directed by your instructor.

Primary Care Skill 4
CPR – Cardiopulmonary Resuscitation
Chest Compressions

Your Goals

▶ Perform adult CPR – chest compressions at a rate of at least 100 chest compressions per minute and depressing the chest approximately one-third the depth of chest – at least 5 cm/2 inches.

▶ Minimize interruptions in chest compressions.

Cycle of Care: AB-CABS™

Continue Until Help or AED Arrives

A B
Airway Open?   Breathing Normally?

C Chest Compressions

A Airway Open

B Breathing for Patient

S Serious Bleeding Shock Spinal Injury

Chest Compressions

Key Points

◆ CPR is a two-step process. Step one – chest compressions are followed by step two – rescue breathing. During this skill, you'll learn step one.

◆ If you are unable or feel uncomfortable giving a patient the rescue breaths – relax. Give the patient immediate and continuous chest compressions. Chest compressions alone are very beneficial to an unresponsive patient who is not breathing normally. Your efforts will still help circulate blood that contains oxygen.

◆ Use the *Cycle of Care* and AB-CABS memory word to help you remember to perform Chest Compressions before opening a patient's Airway and Breathing for the patient.

◆ Give the Responder Statement and tap the patient on the collarbone. If the patient is unresponsive, quickly check for an open airway and normal breathing.

◆ If the patient is not breathing normally, immediately begin Chest Compressions.

◆ The patient must be on his back and on a sturdy surface prior to beginning chest compressions.

◆ Only practice CPR – chest compressions on a mannequin, never on another participant.

Open Airway

Alert EMS

Check Responsiveness

Check for Normal Breathing

How It's Done

1 Assess the scene for safety. Check the patient for responsiveness by giving the Responder Statement: *Hello? My Name is_____. I'm an Emergency Responder. May I help you?* If no response to your statement, then tap the patient on collarbone and ask, *Are you okay? Are you okay?* The collarbone is sensitive and tapping it will reveal a level of responsiveness.

2 Quickly check for an open Airway and normal Breathing.

> **NOTE** – In the first few minutes after cardiac arrest, a patient may be barely breathing, or taking infrequent, noisy, gasps. This is often termed agonal breathing and must not be confused with normal breathing.

3 Alert EMS if the patient is unresponsive and not breathing normally. *Call First* before providing care.

▲ Ask a bystander to call EMS and secure an AED if possible.

▲ If you are alone, use your mobile phone to call EMS.

▲ Leave the patient to call EMS if no other option exists.

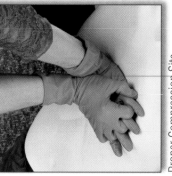

Proper Compression Site

Chest Compressions

4   Position patient on his back (if not already in this position).

5   Locate the chest compression site.

▲   Expose the patient's chest only if necessary to find the compression site.

▲   Find the compression site by putting the heel of one hand in the chest center. On some individuals, this position is between the nipples.

▲   Place your other hand on top of the hand already on the chest and interlock your fingers.

▲   Use the palm of your hand on the compression site. Keep fingers off the chest.

6   Deliver chest compressions.

▲   Position yourself so that your shoulders are directly over your hands and your arms are straight – lock your elbows.

▲   Keep the force of the compressions straight down – avoid pushing on the rib cage or the lower tip of the breastbone. With locked elbows, allow your body weight to deliver the compressions.

▲   To provide effective chest compressions you should push hard and push fast, depressing the breast bone approximately one-third the depth of the patient's chest – at least 5 centimetres/2 inches.

▲   After each chest compression, release, allowing the chest to return to its normal position.

▲   Repeat at a pace of – one-two-three-four – and so on, (counting fast) for 30 compressions. Perform the compressions as fluidly as possible. Your rate should be at least 100 compressions per minute. The rate is a lot faster than most people think – Push Hard, Push Fast.

| TRY IT | In your practice group, perform CPR – chest compressions on a mannequin. One person is the guide, reading the steps, one watches, while the other is the Emergency Responder. First, practice the steps slowly to make sure your hands, arm and body position is appropriate. Next, practice the steps again in real time.

Primary Care Skill 5
CPR – Cardiopulmonary Resuscitation
Chest Compressions Combined With Rescue Breathing

Your Goals

▲ Perform adult complete CPR – chest compressions combined with rescue breathing – at a ratio of 30 chest compressions to 2 rescue breaths.

▲ Minimize interruptions in chest compressions.

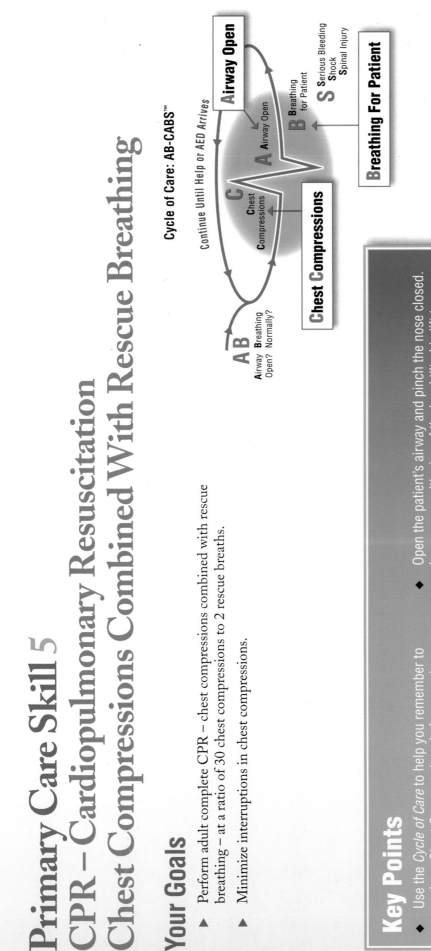

Cycle of Care: AB-CABS™

Continue Until Help or AED Arrives

Airway Open

A Airway Open

B Breathing for Patient

S Serious Bleeding
Shock
Spinal Injury

Breathing For Patient

C Chest Compressions

Chest Compressions

A B
Airway Breathing
Open? Normally?

Key Points

◆ Use the *Cycle of Care* to help you remember to perform Chest Compressions before opening a patient's Airway and Breathing for the patient.

◆ Give the Responder Statement and tap the patient on the collarbone. If the patient is unresponsive, quickly check for an open airway and normal breathing. If the patient is not breathing normally, immediately begin Chest Compressions.

◆ If immediately available, use gloves and a ventilation barrier to protect yourself and patient from disease transmission. However, do not delay providing emergency care by trying to locate barriers.

◆ Open the patient's airway and pinch the nose closed. Improper positioning of the head tilt-chin lift to open an airway is the number one reason rescue breaths are ineffective.

◆ Effective rescue breaths last just over one second, with just enough air to make the patient's chest rise.

◆ If during an actual situation you are unable or feel uncomfortable giving a non-breathing patient rescue breaths, give the patient continuous chest compressions. Chest compressions alone are very beneficial to a patient without a heartbeat. Your efforts may still help circulate blood that contains some oxygen. Remember – adequate care provided is better than perfect care withheld.

Open Airway

Alert EMS

Check Responsiveness

Check for Normal Breathing

Deliver Chest Compressions

How It's Done

1 Assess the scene for safety. Check the patient for responsiveness by giving the Responder Statement: *Hello? My Name is _____ . I'm an Emergency Responder. May I help you?* If no response to your statement, then tap the patient on collarbone and ask, *Are you okay? Are you okay?* The collarbone is sensitive and tapping it will reveal a level of responsiveness.

2 Quickly check for an open Airway and normal Breathing.

3 If the patient is unresponsive and not breathing normally, ask a bystander to call EMS and bring an AED if one is available. If you are alone, use your mobile phone to call EMS. If you do not have a mobile phone, leave the patient to call EMS if no other option exists. This is the *Call First* approach to emergency care. You *Call First* to activate EMS, then you provide assistance.

4 Position patient on his back (if not already in this position).

5 Locate the chest compression site.

▲ Expose the patient's chest only if necessary to find the compression site.

▲ Find the compression site by putting the heel of one hand in the chest center. On some individuals, this position is between the nipples.

▲ Place your other hand on top of the hand already on the chest and interlock your fingers.

▲ Use the palm of your hand on the compression site. Keep fingers off the chest.

6 Deliver chest compressions.

▲ Position yourself so that your shoulders are directly over your hands and your arms are straight – lock your elbows.

▲ Keep the force of the compressions straight down – avoid pushing on the rib cage or the lower tip of the breastbone. Allow your body weight to deliver the compressions.

▲ To provide effective chest compressions you should push hard and push fast, depressing the breast bone approximately one-third the depth of the patient's chest – at least 5 centimeters/2 inches.

▲ After each chest compression, release, allowing the chest to return to its normal position.

▲ Repeat at a pace of – one-two-three-four – and so on, (counting fast) for 30 compressions. Perform the compressions as fluidly as possible. Your rate should be at least 100 compressions per minute. The rate is a lot faster than most people think – Push Hard, Push Fast.

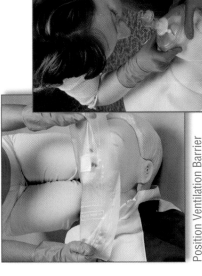

Position Ventilation Barrier

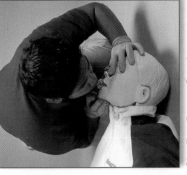

Pocket Mask

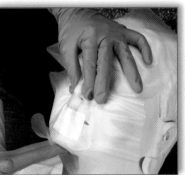

Open Airway and Pinch Nose Closed

Give Two Rescue Breaths

Begin Another Cycle of 30 Chest Compressions

7 Position a ventilation barrier on the mannequin for mouth-to-mouth or mouth-to-mask rescue breaths.

8 Open the patient's airway. Use ONE of two common methods – head tilt-chin lift or pistol grip.

NOTE – If patient has an injury to the face or jaw, gently close the mouth to protect the injured site. While holding the jaw closed, place your mouth over the barrier covering the nose and give rescue breaths through the nose. Certain ventilation barriers (such as a pocket mask) are better for mouth-to-nose than others. Using a pocket mask is another form of rescue breathing called mouth-to-mask.

9 With the patient's head tilted back and the ventilation barrier in place, pinch the nose closed.

10 Now, give two rescue breaths. Each breath should last about one second. Provide the patient with just enough air to make the patient's chest rise. Look for this rise in the patient's chest.

▶ If you can't make the patient's chest rise with the first breath, repeat the head tilt-chin lift or pistol grip lift to re-open the airway before attempting another breath. Improperly opening a patient's airway is the most common cause of not being able to inflate a patient's lungs.

NOTE – Do not try more than twice to give rescue breaths that make the chest rise. Minimize delay between chest compressions. After two breaths, whether they make the chest rise or not, begin chest compressions again.

11 After delivering two rescue breaths, immediately begin another cycle of 30 chest compressions. Minimize delays in providing chest compressions.

12 Continue alternating 30 compressions with two breaths until:

▶ EMS arrives.

▶ You can defibrillate with an AED (Automated External Defibrillator).

▶ The patient becomes responsive and begins to breathe normally.

▶ Another Emergency Responder takes over CPR efforts.

▶ You are too exhausted to continue.

Avoid CPR Fatigue - Alternate Care Between Two Rescuers

NOTE – If more than one Emergency Responder is present consider alternating care. To avoid fatigue, each provider can deliver CPR for two minutes and then switch. While switching providers, minimize chest compression interruptions.

NOTE – If the patient's problem could be a drowning or other respiratory problem, give *Care First*. This means that you provide CPR to the patient for a *short time* and THEN call EMS.

Two national guidelines define providing *Care First* for a *short time* differently. In North, South and Central America, Asia and the Pacific Island countries (AHA Guidelines), it's defined as providing care for approximately two minutes; the European Resuscitation Council guidelines defines a *short time* as one minute.

TRY IT

In your practice groups, perform CPR – chest compressions combined with rescue breathing on a mannequin. One person is the guide, reading the steps, one watches, while the other is the Emergency Responder. First, practice the steps slowly to make sure your hands, arm and body position is appropriate. Next, practice the steps again in real time.

Optional Primary Care Skill
Automated External Defibrillator Use

Your Goals

Demonstrate how to:

▲ Use an Automated External Defibrillator (AED) on a mannequin according to the machine manufacturer's guidelines.

▲ Place AED pads on a patient with no signs of circulation.

▲ Assist a patient who has been successfully defibrillated with an AED.

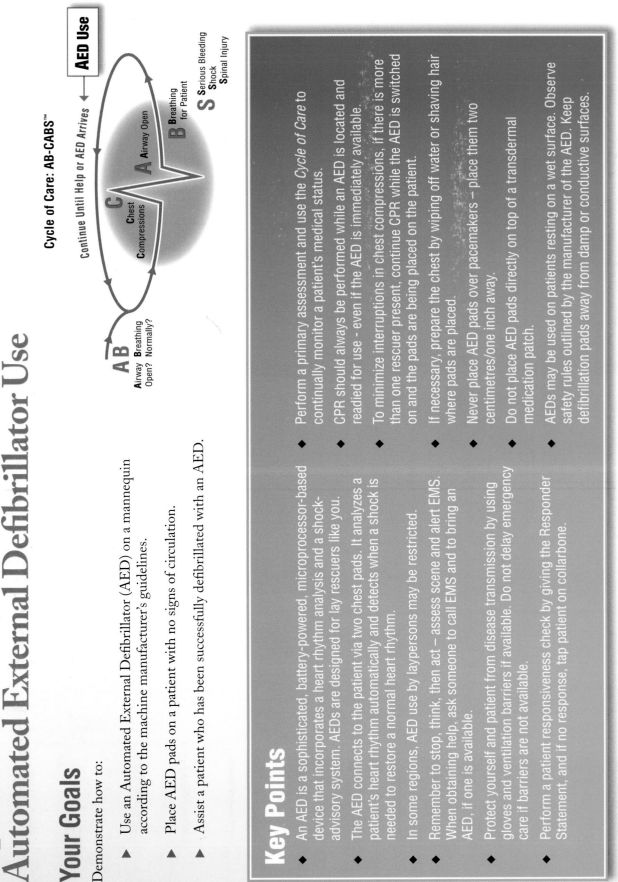

Cycle of Care: AB-CABS™

Continue Until Help or AED Arrives → **AED Use**

AB
Airway Breathing
Open? Normally?

C Chest Compressions

A Airway Open

B Breathing for Patient

S Serious Bleeding
Shock
Spinal Injury

Key Points

◆ An AED is a sophisticated, battery-powered, microprocessor-based device that incorporates a heart rhythm analysis and a shock-advisory system. AEDs are designed for lay rescuers like you.

◆ The AED connects to the patient via two chest pads. It analyzes a patient's heart rhythm automatically and detects when a shock is needed to restore a normal heart rhythm.

◆ In some regions, AED use by laypersons may be restricted.

◆ Remember to stop, think, then act – assess scene and alert EMS. When obtaining help, ask someone to call EMS and to bring an AED, if one is available.

◆ Protect yourself and patient from disease transmission by using gloves and ventilation barriers if available. Do not delay emergency care if barriers are not available.

◆ Perform a patient responsiveness check by giving the Responder Statement, and if no response, tap patient on collarbone.

◆ Perform a primary assessment and use the *Cycle of Care* to continually monitor a patient's medical status.

◆ CPR should always be performed while an AED is located and readied for use - even if the AED is immediately available.

◆ To minimize interruptions in chest compressions, if there is more than one rescuer present, continue CPR while the AED is switched on and the pads are being placed on the patient.

◆ If necessary, prepare the chest by wiping off water or shaving hair where pads are placed.

◆ Never place AED pads over pacemakers – place them two centimetres/one inch away.

◆ Do not place AED pads directly on top of a transdermal medication patch.

◆ AEDs may be used on patients resting on a wet surface. Observe safety rules outlined by the manufacturer of the AED. Keep defibrillation pads away from damp or conductive surfaces.

Begin CPR

Call EMS

Turn AED On - Follow Prompts

Bystander Brings AED

You may have an orientation to an AED as an optional skill in the Emergency First Response Primary Care (CPR) course.

Permission for use of image(s) granted by Cardiac Science Corp., www.cardiacscience.com and www.cardiacscience.de

An AED delivers a shock to a patient who is not breathing and has no heartbeat.

How It's Done

1   Use the *Cycle of Care* to continually monitor the patient's medical status.

2   If the patient is unresponsive and not breathing normally, first call EMS or have a bystander call and bring an AED. Next, immediately begin CPR.

▶   If you are alone and know where to find an AED close by, continue CPR for a couple of minutes then leave the patient to quickly secure the AED.

▶   If a bystander can go get an AED, direct them to do so while you begin or continue CPR. Once the person arrives with the AED, have them set it up and place the chest pads on the patient while you continue CPR. This minimizes interruptions to chest compressions.

3   Position the AED close to the patient's ear on the same side as the rescuer.

4   Turn AED power ON – follow device prompts exactly.

5   Bare the patient's chest. If the patient is wet, consider drying the chest prior to pad placement. It is not uncommon for a razor to be included with an AED. If available, use it quickly to shave excessive body hair.

6   Remove defibrillator pads from packaging – peel away any protective plastic backing from the pads.

NOTE – The following steps are generic and universal. Please refer to the manufacturer guidelines and instructions when using a specific AED.

Place Defibrillator Pads

Clear Rescuers and Bystanders

Provide a Shock

Resume CPR

7   As directed by the manufacturer, place defibrillator pads on patient's bare chest, adhesive side down (note placement illustrations on pad packaging or pads). Typically:

   ▲   One pad goes on the upper-right side of the chest, below the collarbone and next to the breastbone.

   ▲   One pad goes on the lower-left side of the chest, to the left and below the nipple line.

8   Plug in AED if needed or prompted. AED will analyze the patient's heart rhythm. (Some AEDs require you to push an Analyze button.)

9   Clear rescuers and bystanders from the patient making sure no one is touching the patient. Also, make sure no equipment is touching the patient. Say, *I'm clear, you are clear, everyone is clear.*

10 If the AED advises that a shock is needed, the responder should follow the prompts to provide one shock, followed by CPR. If the AED does not advise a shock, immediately resume CPR.

11 The AED will again analyze the patient's heart rhythm. If normal breathing is still absent, the AED may prompt you to deliver another shock. Most AEDs will wait two minutes before analyzing and shocking the patient again. During that time, continue CPR.

12 As prompted, continue to give single shocks combined with CPR until the patient resumes breathing, until relieved by EMS personnel, or until you are physically unable to continue.

13 If the patient begins breathing normally, support the open airway and continue to use the *Cycle of Care* to monitor the patient's medical status.

TRY IT

In your practice group, place AED pads on a mannequin and proceed through the Analyze and Shock steps. One person is the guide, reading the steps, one watches, while the other is the Emergency Responder. Each Emergency Responder should:

   ●   Practice AED pad placement.

   ◉   Practice on an AED Trainer or simulate the steps for analyzing and shocking a patient (mannequin).

Make sure everyone has the chance to act as the Emergency Responder. Alter circumstances as directed by your instructor.

Primary Care Skill 6
Serious Bleeding Management

Your Goal

Demonstrate how to use sustained direct pressure and a pressure bandage to manage a serious bleeding wound.

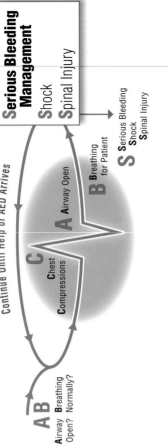

Cycle of Care: AB-CABS™

Continue Until Help or AED Arrives

A Airway Open
B Breathing for Patient
C Chest Compressions

A B
Airway Open? Breathing Normally?

S Serious Bleeding Shock Spinal Injury

Serious Bleeding Management
Shock
Spinal Injury

→ Serious Bleeding Shock Spinal Injury

Key Points

◆ Remember to stop, think, then act – assess scene and alert EMS.

◆ Use barriers appropriately. For serious bleeding, appropriate barriers include gloves, eye shield, and personal facemask. Protect yourself and patient from disease transmission by using gloves and barriers.

◆ Perform a patient responsiveness check by giving the Responder Statement, and if no response, tap patient on collarbone.

◆ Perform a primary assessment – remember bleeding must be severe to be life-threatening. Use the *Cycle of Care* to continually monitor a patient's medical status.

◆ Reassure the patient as you treat for bleeding.

◆ Assist patient into a position of comfort while treating.

◆ Keep in mind that direct pressure is the first and most successful method for serious bleeding management.

◆ Using a pressure bandage is the next step to control bleeding. A pressure bandage is anything that places constant direct pressure on a wound.

Australia and New Zealand Resuscitation Council Specific Key Points

◆ To assist in controlling bleeding, where possible: 1) Elevate the bleeding part. 2) Restrict patient movement. 3) Immobilize the part. 4) Advise the victim to remain at total rest.

◆ Administer oxygen if available.

◆ Do not give patient anything orally, including medications and/or alcohol.

◆ For an embedded object: 1) Do not remove object as it can restrict bleeding. 2) Use indirect pressure by placing padding around or above/below the object and apply pressure over the pads.

◆ As a last resort and only when other methods of controlling bleeding have failed, a tourniquet may be applied to a limb to control life-threatening bleeding (e.g., traumatic amputation of a limb or injuries with massive blood loss). Tourniquet should be at least 5 cm/2 inches wide, placed high above the bleeding point and tightened to stop bleeding. Time of application should be noted. See *Emergency Reference* section for step-by-step procedure.

Release Pressure Periodically

Bandage Rather Tightly

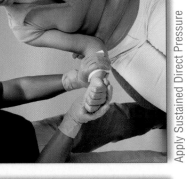

Apply Sustained Direct Pressure

Use Pressure Bandage

Put on Barriers

How It's Done

Direct Pressure

1 Give Emergency Responder statement. Assess scene, alert EMS and make sure airway is open.

2 Put on barriers – gloves, eye shields, and facemask as appropriate.

3 Place a clean cloth or a sterile dressing over wound and apply sustained direct pressure. If a dressing or cloth is not available, use gloved hand.

4 Release pressure periodically to determine if bleeding has slowed or stopped.

Pressure Bandage

1 While applying direct pressure on wound, place a pressure bandage over the sterile dressing.

2 If bandage becomes blood-soaked, place another clean cloth or dressing on top and bandage in place.

3 Continue to apply direct pressure to wound.

4 Don't remove blood-soaked bandages because blood clots in the dressing help control bleeding. Add bandages as necessary. (There may be country specific protocols for direction on when to remove bandages.)

5 Bandage rather tightly – avoiding total restriction of blood flow (no discoloring of fingers or toes). Keep the pressure bandage flat against wound – avoid allowing the bandage to twist into a small string.

TRY IT

In your practice group begin by performing a primary assessment and attend to an imaginary serious bleeding wound on a patient's arm. Use direct pressure on the wound, and apply a pressure bandage. One person is the guide, reading the steps, one acts as a patient with a wound, while the other is the Emergency Responder.

Make sure everyone has the chance to act as the Emergency Responder. Alter circumstances as directed by your instructor.

Primary Care Skill 7
Shock Management

Your Goal

Demonstrate how to manage shock by conducting a primary assessment, protecting the patient and stabilizing the head.

Cycle of Care: AB-CABS™

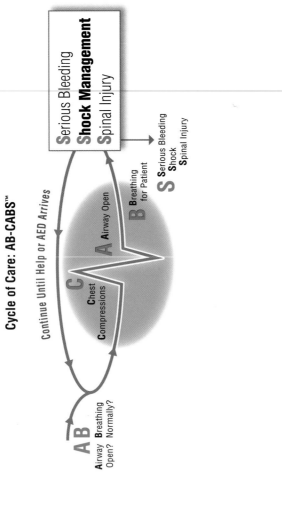

Continue Until Help or AED Arrives

A Airway Open?
B Breathing Normally?

C Chest Compressions
A Airway Open
B Breathing for Patient

S Serious Bleeding
Shock
Spinal Injury

Serious Bleeding
Shock Management
Spinal Injury

Key Points

◆ Remember to stop, think, then act – assess scene and alert EMS.

◆ Protect yourself and patient from disease transmission by using gloves and barriers if available. Do not delay emergency care if barriers are not available.

◆ Perform a patient responsiveness check by giving the Responder Statement, and if no response, tap patient on collarbone.

◆ Perform a primary assessment and use the *Cycle of Care* to continually monitor a patient's medical status.

◆ Shock results when an injury or illness makes it difficult for the body's cardiovascular system to provide adequate amounts of oxygenated blood to vital organs.

◆ Always treat an injured or ill patient for shock even if signs and symptoms are absent.

◆ For a responsive patient, let the patient determine what position is most comfortable – sitting, lying down, etc. Unresponsive patients could be placed in the recovery position.

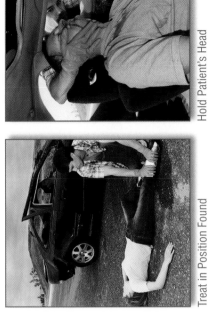

Treat in Position Found

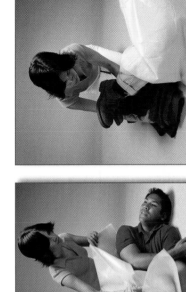

Hold Patient's Head

Elevate Legs

Maintain Body Temperature

How It's Done

1 Treat an injured, unresponsive or unconscious patient in the position found. Do not move if possible.

2 Hold the patient's head to keep the neck from moving.

3 Maintain patient's body temperature based on local climate. This may mean covering the patient with a blanket or exposure protection from the sun.

4 If there are no spinal injuries or leg fractures suspected, elevate the legs 15-30 centimetres/6-12 inches to allow blood to return to the heart.

TRY IT

In your practice group, begin by performing a primary assessment and manage shock for an unconscious patient laying on the floor. Cover with a blanket or shade the patient to provide a normal temperature. Elevate the patient's legs 15–30 centimetres/6–12 inches. One person is the guide, reading the steps, one acts as a patient with shock, while the other is the Emergency Responder. Be resourceful, use items in the room to shade or cover patient and elevate legs.

Make sure everyone has the chance to act as the Emergency Responder. Alter circumstances as directed by your instructor.

Primary Care Skill 8
Spinal Injury Management

Your Goal

Demonstrate how to manage a suspected spinal injury by conducting a primary assessment, protecting the patient and stabilizing the head. Demonstrate how to place a patient on his back by performing a log roll to minimize spine and neck movement.

Cycle of Care: AB-CABS™

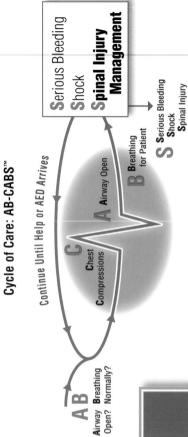

Continue Until Help or AED Arrives

C Chest Compressions
A Airway Open
B Breathing for Patient
S Serious Bleeding Shock Spinal Injury

AB Airway Open? Breathing Normally?

Serious Bleeding
Shock
Spinal Injury Management

→ Serious Bleeding Shock Spinal Injury

Stabilize Head

Key Points

♦ Remember to stop, think, then act – assess scene and alert EMS.

♦ Protect yourself and patient from disease transmission by using gloves and barriers if available. Do not delay emergency care if barriers are not available.

♦ Perform a patient responsiveness check by giving the Responder Statement, and if no response, tap patient on collarbone.

♦ Suspect a spinal injury for any incident involving a fall, severe blow, crash or other strong impact. Also suspect spinal injury if a patient complains of back or neck pain or can't move an arm or leg.

♦ If possible, perform primary assessment in the position the patient is found. Do not move patient unless safety is in question. Use the *Cycle of Care* to continually monitor a patient's medical status.

How It's Done

For a responsive patient who is breathing normally

1 Stabilize head by placing a hand on each side to prevent movement. Attempt to anchor your arms or elbows on the ground or use a similar stable position to assist with minimizing your hand movement.

2 Instruct patient to remain still and not move his head or neck while waiting for EMS to arrive.

For an unresponsive patient who is not breathing normally:

1 To open the airway, assess breathing and administer CPR, the patient must be on his back.

▲ If patient is already on back, use the head tilt-chin lift method to open the patient's airway. Minimize overall head movement, and do not tilt from side to side.

▲ If the patient is not on his back, use the log roll to reposition patient.

2 To perform a log roll by yourself:

▲ Kneel at the patient's side. Leave enough room so that the patient will not roll into your lap.

▲ Gently straighten the patient's legs. Straighten arms against side of patient.

▲ Cradle the patient's head and neck from behind with one of your hands.

▲ Place your other hand on the patient's elbow, on the patient's arm that is furthest away from you.

▲ Roll the patient carefully as a unit, head and body together toward you, onto the side, then onto the back.

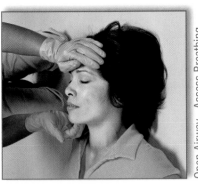

Open Airway - Assess Breathing

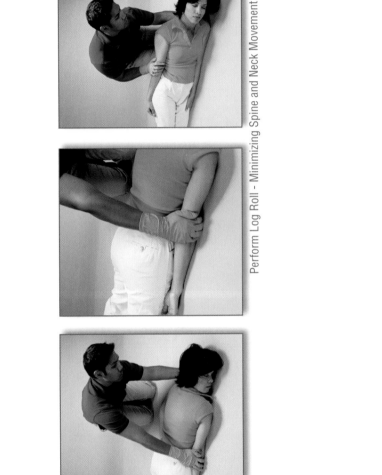

Perform Log Roll - Minimizing Spine and Neck Movement

SKILLS WORKBOOK

2-25

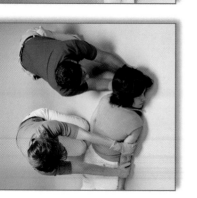

Two–Person Log Roll

3   If help is available, perform a two–person log roll:

▲   One Emergency Responder stabilizes patient's head, one rolls patient. Patient's head is stabilized with both hands to keep it from moving.

▲   Emergency Responder rolling patient, does so with both hands on patient's arm above and below elbow.

▲   Both responders roll patient as one unit onto patient's back.

TRY IT

In your practice group, begin by performing a primary assessment on a responsive patient with a suspected spinal injury. Next, practice a log roll and primary assessment on an unconscious and unresponsive patient with a suspected spinal injury who is positioned face down.

If practical, practice both two–person and one–person log rolls. One person is the guide, reading the steps, one acts as a patient with a suspected spinal injury, while the other is the Emergency Responder.

Make sure everyone has the chance to act as the Emergency Responder. Alter circumstances as directed by your instructor.

Primary Care Skill 9
Conscious and Unconscious Choking Adult

NOTE – Procedures for handling a conscious choking patient vary internationally. You will learn the protocols appropriate for your area. This skill includes variations based on three different guideline procedures. The different procedures come from the American Heart Association used in North, South and Central America, Asia and the Pacific Island countries (AHA Guidelines), European Resuscitation Council (ERC), plus Australian and New Zealand Resuscitation Council (ARC/NZRC).

Performance Requirement

Demonstrate how to assist a conscious and unconscious choking patient with a partial or complete (severe) airway obstruction.

Cycle of Care: AB-CABS™

Continue Until Help or AED Arrives

C Chest Compressions
A Airway Open
B Breathing for Patient
S Serious Bleeding / Shock / Spinal Injury

A Airway Open?
B Breathing Normally?

Breathing Normally?

Key Points

- Remember to stop, think, then act.
- If the patient is coughing, wheezing or can speak, observe until the patient expels the obstruction. Reassure and encourage the patient to keep coughing to expel the foreign material.
- Remember that a conscious adult must give consent before you do anything. A head nod is sufficient.
- If the blockage is severe, the patient will not be able to cough.
- Perform chest thrusts on pregnant or obese individuals rather than abdominal thrust.
- Patients who receive the treatment for conscious choking should be medically evaluated to rule out any life-threatening complications.

SKILLS WORKBOOK

2-27

SKILLS WORKBOOK

Abdominal Thrusts

Locate Navel - Belly Button

Stand Behind Patient

Make a Fist

Place Other Hand Over Fist

Perform Inward - Upward Thrusts

Conscious Choking Chest Thrusts

Bend Arms/Elbows Outward

Conscious Choking Adult – AHA Guidelines (North, South and Central America, Asia and the Pacific Island countries)

How It's Done

1 Start by asking a responsive patient – *"Are you choking?"*

2 If the patient cannot speak or is not breathing normally, give the Responder Statement *"Hello? My name is _____. I'm an Emergency Responder. May I help you?"*

3 When permission is granted (a head nod is sufficient), alert EMS and proceed with attempts to dislodge the object.

4 Consider chest thrusts if abdominal thrusts are not effective. Begin with chest thrusts on patients who are pregnant or markedly obese.

Conscious Choking Abdominal Thrusts

1 Stand behind the patient and place your arms around waist.

2 Locate the patient's navel (belly button) – the thrust site is two finger widths above it.

3 Make a fist and place the thumb side on the thrust site.

4 Place your other hand over the outside of the fist.

5 Bend your arms and elbows outward to avoid squeezing the rib cage.

6 Perform quick inward and upward thrusts until the obstruction is cleared or the patient becomes unconscious.

7 Once the obstruction is cleared, encourage the patient to breathe and monitor the patient.

Conscious Choking Chest Thrusts

1 Stand behind the patient and place your arms around body, under armpits.

2 Follow the lowest rib upward until you reach the point where the ribs meet in the center.

3 Feel the notch on the lower half of the breastbone, sternum, and place your middle and index finger on the notch. This is the same compression point as for CPR.

4 Make a fist and place the thumb side on the thrust site above your fingers on the notch.

5 Place the other hand over the outside of the fist.

6 Perform quick inward thrusts until the object is expelled or the patient becomes unconscious.

7 Avoid putting pressure on the rib cage.

8 Stop if the obstruction clears, encourage the patient to breathe and monitor the patient.

Conscious Choking Adult – European Resuscitation Council (ERC) Guidelines

How It's Done

1 Start by asking a responsive patient – *"Are you choking?"*

2 If the patient cannot speak or is not breathing normally, give the Responder Statement *"Hello? My name is _____. I'm an Emergency Responder. May I help you?"*

3 When permission is granted (a head nod is sufficient), alert EMS and proceed with attempts to dislodge the object.

4 Begin with back blows then move to abdominal thrusts. Alternate back blows with abdominal thrusts until the obstruction is cleared or the patient becomes unconscious.

Conscious Choking Back Blows

1 To deliver back blows, take a position to the side and slightly behind the patient.

2 Support the chest with one hand, and lean the patient forward.

3 Firmly strike the person between the shoulder blades with the heel of the other hand five times.

4 If five back blows do not clear the obstruction, switch to abdominal thrusts.

5 Stop if the obstruction clears, encourage the patient to breathe and monitor the patient.

Conscious Choking Abdominal Thrusts

1 Stand behind the patient and place both arms round the upper part of the abdomen.

2 Lean the patient forward.

3 Clench your fist and place it between the navel (belly button) and the ribcage.

4 Grasp this hand with your other hand and pull sharply inwards and upwards.

5 Repeat five times.

6 If five abdominal thrusts do not clear the obstruction, switch to back blows.

7 Stop if the obstruction clears, encourage the patient to breathe and monitor the patient.

Firmly Deliver Back Blows

Position Yourself to the Side and Behind Patient

Make a Fist

Locate Belly Button

Bend Arms/Elbows Outward

Perform Inward - Upward Thrusts

Stand Behind Patient

Place Other Hand Over Fist

Conscious Choking Adult – Australia and New Zealand Resuscitation Council (ARC/NZRC) Guidelines

How It's Done

1 Start by asking a responsive patient – *"Are you choking?"*

2 If the patient cannot speak or is not breathing normally, give the Responder Statement *"Hello? My name is _____. I'm an Emergency Responder. May I help you?"*

3 When permission is granted (a head nod is sufficient), alert EMS and proceed with attempts to dislodge the object.

4 Begin with back blows then move to chest thrusts. Alternate back blows with chest thrusts until the obstruction is cleared or the patient becomes unconscious.

Conscious Choking Back Blows

1 To deliver back blows, take a position to the side and slightly behind the patient.

2 Support the chest with one hand, and lean the patient forward.

3 Firmly strike the person between the shoulder blades with the heel of the other hand up to five times. The aim is to relieve the obstruction with each blow rather than to give all five blows. Stop if the obstruction clears, encourage the patient to breathe and monitor the patient.

4 If five back blows do not clear the obstruction, switch to chest thrusts.

Conscious Choking Chest Thrusts

1 Stand behind the patient and place your arms around body, under armpits.

2 Follow the lowest rib upward until you reach the point where the ribs meet in the center.

3 Feel the notch on the lower half of the breastbone (sternum) and place your middle and index finger on the notch.

4 Make a fist and place the thumb side on the thrust site above your fingers on the notch. This is the same compression point as for CPR.

5 Place the other hand over the outside of the fist.

6 Perform up to five quick inward thrusts. Avoid putting pressure on the rib cage.

7 The aim is to relieve the obstruction with each chest thrust rather than to give all five chest thrusts. Stop if the obstruction clears, encourage the patient to breathe and monitor the patient.

Firmly Deliver Back Blows

Position Yourself to the Side and Behind Patient

Conscious Choking Chest Thrusts

Unconscious Choking Patient – Used in All Regions

1 If a responsive, choking patient becomes unconscious while you are trying to help, carefully help the unconscious patient to the ground.

2 Activate EMS if not already called.

3 Begin CPR as per Primary Care Skill 5.

4 Following chest compressions, quickly look in the patient's mouth and attempt to remove any visible obstruction. If an object is seen, you should remove the object with your finger.

5 If no object is seen or the object has been removed, proceed with two rescue breaths.

6 Continue CPR until obstruction is relieved or EMS arrives.

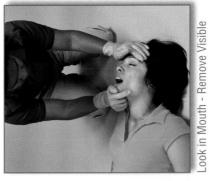

Look in Mouth - Remove Visible Obstruction

Rescue Breaths

Activate EMS - Begin CPR

TRY IT

In your practice group, perform the steps to assist a conscious choking patient. One person is the guide, reading the steps, one is the patient, while the other is the Emergency Responder. Make sure everyone has the chance to act as the Emergency Responder.

Remember – Do not actually perform thrusts or blows on another participant during practice.

Next, discuss and/or perform the steps for assisting a patient who has become unconscious from a choking incident. Your instructor will direct you. Alter circumstances as directed by your instructor.

Recommended Primary Care Skill
Emergency Oxygen Use – Orientation

Your Goal

Demonstrate how to administer emergency oxygen to a patient with a serious or life-threatening illness or injury.

How It's Done

1 Follow system instructions to set up oxygen unit.

2 Always turn valve on slowly and test that oxygen is flowing to mask.

3 For a responsive patient, ask if you may provide oxygen and place mask over the patient's mouth and nose. Say, *This is oxygen, may I place this mask on you?* Responder takes first breath from mask, but does not exhale.

Cycle of Care: AB-CABS™

Continue Until Help or AED Arrives

A B Airway Breathing Open? Normally?

C Chest Compressions

A Airway Open

B Breathing for Patient

S Serious Bleeding Shock Spinal Injury

Breathing Normally?
Assist with use of Emergency Oxygen.

Key Points

◆ Remember to stop, think, then act – assess scene and alert EMS.

◆ Protect yourself and patient from disease transmission by using gloves and barriers if available. Do not delay emergency care if barriers are not available.

◆ Perform a patient responsiveness check by giving the Responder Statement, and if no response, tap patient on collarbone.

◆ Perform a primary assessment and use the *Cycle of Care* to continually monitor a patient's medical status.

◆ Become familiar with the emergency oxygen units that you may need to use before you need to use them – at home, work, school, etc.

◆ Use emergency oxygen in a ventilated area away from any source of flame or heat.

◆ Handle oxygen cylinder carefully because contents are under high pressure. Avoid dropping cylinder or exposing it to heat.

◆ Emergency oxygen is appropriate treatment for near drowning, scuba diving incidents and heart attacks.

◆ In some regions, oxygen use is restricted.

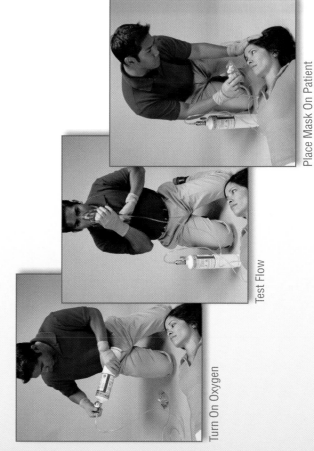

Turn On Oxygen

Test Flow

Place Mask On Patient

Monitor Oxygen Gauge

Patient Holds Mask

Rescue Breaths with Added Oxygen

▶ If the patient agrees, have the patient hold the mask in place and tell the patient to breathe normally.

▶ If the patient can't hold the mask, use the strap to keep it in place.

4 For an unresponsive, breathing patient, place mask on patient's nose and mouth and secure with strap.

5 For an unconscious, non-breathing patient, use a mask that allows you to supply rescue breaths while oxygen flows into mask.

6 Monitor oxygen unit pressure gauge to avoid emptying it while the mask is still on the patient.

7 Additional training in administering emergency oxygen may be required in some regions.

TRY IT

In your practice group, set up an oxygen unit following your instructor's directions. Next, perform a primary assessment on a responsive patient. One person is the guide, reading the steps, one is the patient, while the other is the Emergency Responder. Offer patient emergency oxygen following your instructor's directions.

Make sure everyone has the chance to act as the Emergency Responder. Alter circumstances as directed by your instructor.

Secondary Care First Aid

Secondary Care Skill 1
Injury Assessment

Your Goal

Demonstrate how to conduct a head-to-toe injury assessment on a patient and note injuries to report to Emergency Medical Service (EMS) personnel.

Key Points

♦ Use this skill to determine what first aid may be needed in the event of any injury – especially when EMS is either delayed or unavailable.

♦ Remember to stop, think, then act – assess scene and alert EMS if necessary.

♦ Protect yourself and patient from disease transmission by using gloves and barriers if available. Do not delay emergency care if barriers are not available.

♦ Perform a patient responsiveness check by giving the Responder Statement, and if no response, tap patient on collarbone.

♦ Perform a primary assessment and use the *Cycle of Care* to continually monitor a patient's medical status.

♦ Only perform injury assessments on conscious, responsive patients.

♦ When possible, perform the assessment in the position the patient is found.

♦ If wound dressings are in place, do not remove during the assessment.

♦ Look for wounds, bleeding, discolorations or deformities.

♦ Listen for unusual breathing sounds.

♦ Feel for swelling or hardness, tissue softness, unusual masses, joint tenderness, deformities and changes in body temperature. Make mental notes of the assessment and report findings to EMS personnel.

♦ Avoid giving injured patient anything to eat or drink, as he may need surgery.

Stabilize Head

Ask Permission to Assist

Check Ears

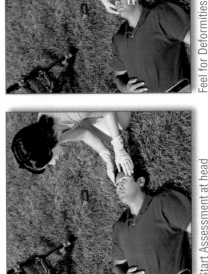
Feel for Deformities

Start Assessment at head

How It's Done

1 Deliver Responder Statement, asking permission to assist. Give a brief explanation of what you'll be doing during the assessment. Put on gloves.

2 Stabilize patient's head and instruct patient to answer verbally. Do not allow patient to move or nod head.

3 Immediately stop assessment if patient complains of head, neck or back pain. Continue to stabilize head and neck – ending assessment and waiting for EMS to arrive. Do not move.

4 Start assessment at head and work your way down body to toes.

5 Feel for deformities on patient's face by gently running your fingers over forehead, cheeks and chin.

6 Check ears and nose for blood or fluid. If present, suspect head injury and stop further assessment.

Check Eyes

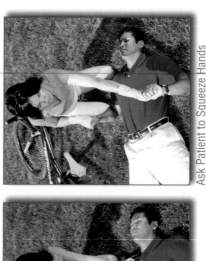

Check Shoulder Blades

Check Eyes

Feel Neck for Abnormalities

Ask Patient to Squeeze Hands

Check Arms

Check Collarbone

Check Shoulders

7   Place a finger in front of patient's eyes. Without moving the head, have patient follow your finger with his eyes. Check eyes for smooth tracking. Eyes should move together. If possible, check pupil size and reaction to light.

8   Feel skull and neck for abnormalities. If patient complains of pain, stop assessment.

9   If you can reach the shoulder blades, slide or place one hand over each shoulder blade and gently push inwards.

10 Move hands outward to shoulders and press gently inward with palm.

11 Run two fingers over the collarbones from shoulders to center.

12 Place one hand on shoulder to stabilize arm. Gently slide other hand down the upper arm, elbow and wrist. Repeat on other arm. Ask patient to wiggle fingers on both hands and squeeze your hands.

Check Spinal Column

Check Hipbones

Press Foot Against Hand

Inspect Chest

Check Abdomen

Check Thighs - Legs

13 Inspect chest for deformity. Place a hand, palm in, on each side of patient's rib cage and gently push inward.

14 Gently put your hands under patient to feel the spinal column. Cover as much area as possible without moving patient. Gently touch along the patient's spine, feeling for abnormalities.

15 Using one hand, gently push on patient's abdomen. Apply gentle pressure to right and left side of abdomen, and above and below navel (belly button).

16 Move hands gently over the hipbones to check for swelling or hardness, tissue softness, unusual masses, joint tenderness, and deformities. Avoid pushing inward on hips.

17 Starting at the thigh, slide hand down the upper leg, knee, lower leg and ankle. Ask patient to wiggle toes and press sole of the foot against your hand. Repeat on other leg.

18 Note areas of pain or abnormality for report to EMS personnel. Continue to monitor the patient by using the *Cycle of Care*. Use the Injury Assessment Record Sheet at the end of the *Reference Section*.

TRY IT

In your practice group, perform a primary assessment on a responsive patient. Next, begin your Injury Assessment. In this situation, EMS is either delayed or unavailable.

One person is the guide, reading the steps, one is the patient, while the other is the Emergency Responder. Each patient should think of an imaginary injury. Do not share this imaginary injury with the Emergency Responder. As the Emergency Responder performs his Injury Assessment, act out the injury.

Make sure everyone has the chance to act as the Emergency Responder. Alter circumstances as directed by your instructor.

Secondary Care Skill 2
Illness Assessment

Your Goal

Demonstrate how to conduct an illness assessment by:

▲ Asking how a patient feels and obtaining information about a patient's medical history.

▲ Checking a patient's respirations, pulse rate, temperature, skin moisture and color.

▲ Reporting findings to Emergency Medical Service (EMS) personnel.

Key Points

◆ Use this skill to gather information and determine what first aid may be needed in the event of any illness — especially when EMS is either delayed or unavailable.

◆ Stop, think, then act — assess scene and alert EMS if necessary.

◆ Protect yourself and patient from disease transmission by using gloves and barriers if available. Do not delay emergency care if barriers are not available.

◆ Perform a patient responsiveness check by giving the Responder Statement, and if no response, tap patient on collarbone.

◆ Perform a primary assessment and use the *Cycle of Care* to continually monitor a patient's medical status.

◆ Only perform illness assessments on conscious, responsive patients.

◆ When giving information to EMS personnel, avoid using the word *normal*. Provide measured rates per minute and descriptive terminology.

◆ Use the memory word SAMPLE to remember how to conduct an illness assessment. SAMPLE stands for Signs and Symptoms, Allergies, Medications, Preexisting medical history, Last meal and Events.

◆ Signs are something you see is wrong with a patient. Symptoms are something the patient *tells* you is wrong.

◆ To help guide your assessment, remember that:

↑ The average breathing rate for adults is between 12 and 20 breaths per minute. A patient who takes less than eight breaths per minute, or more than 24 breaths per minute, probably needs immediate medical care.

↑ The average pulse rate for adults is between 60 and 80 beats per minute.

↑ Average skin temperature is warm and skin should feel dry to the touch.

↑ Noticeable skin color changes may indicate heart, lung or circulation problems.

↑ By conducting an illness assessment on a healthy person in class, you will be able to recognize differences later when you assist an unhealthy person.

◆ If a patient complains of chest discomfort or pain call EMS immediately and encourage patient to:

↑ Take any prescribed medication for such discomfort, or

↑ Chew 1 adult, non-coated aspirin (unless patient has an allergy or other contraindication to aspirin).

Checking Carotid Pulse

How It's Done

1 Find a paper and a pen/pencil to record illness assessment information. Use the Illness Assessment Record Sheet at the end of the *Reference* section.

2 If possible, get someone else to record information while you attend to the patient.

3 Put on gloves when needed.

SAMPLE – Signs and Symptoms

1 Ask how patient is feeling and what occurred immediately before the onset of illness. Questions may include:

▲ How do you feel now?

▲ What were you doing when you began to feel ill?

▲ When did the first symptoms occur?

▲ Where were you when the first symptoms occurred?

Finding Pulse Rate

2 To find pulse rate using the carotid artery:

▲ Locate the patient's Adam's apple with the index and middle fingers of one hand.

▲ Slide the fingers down into the groove of the neck on the side closest to you.

▲ If you can't find the pulse on the side closest to you, move to the opposite side.

▲ Never try to feel the carotid pulse on both sides at the same time.

▲ Count the number of beats in 30 seconds and multiply by two to determine the heartbeats per minute.

Checking Radial Artery Pulse

Counting Respirations

3 **To find pulse rate using the radial artery:**

▲ Locate artery on patient's wrist, thumb side of hand.

▲ Slide two or three fingers into the groove of the wrist immediately below the hand on the thumb side.

▲ Do not use your thumb when taking a radial pulse.

▲ Count the number of beats in 30 seconds and multiply by two to determine the heartbeats per minute.

4 Determine whether the pulse may be described as rapid, strong or weak.

Checking Respiration

5 Look for signs and symptoms of respiratory distress, including:

▲ Wheezing, gurgling or high-pitched noises when the patient breathes.

▲ Patient complains of shortness of breath or is feeling dizzy or lightheaded.

▲ Patient complains of pain in the chest and numbness or tingling in arms or legs.

6 To count the number of times a patient breathes, use one of two methods:

▲ **First Method:** Simply watch patient's chest rise and fall and count the respirations.

▲ **Second Method:** If you cannot see the patient's chest rise and fall, place hand on the patient's abdomen. This position allows you to mask your efforts to obtain a count of the patient's respirations. Patients often alter their breathing rate if they become aware their breaths are being counted.

▲ For both methods, count patient's respirations for 30 seconds and multiply by two to determine respiratory rate.

7 Determine whether respirations may be described as fast, slow, labored, wheezing or gasping.

Checking Temperature - Moisture

Epinephrine (Adrenalin) Autoinjector Use

Checking temperature and moisture

8 Feel patient's forehead or cheek with the back of your hand. Compare with your own temperature using your other hand on your forehead. Verify if the patient has perhaps been doing physical exercise.

9 Determine whether the skin is warm, hot, cool, moist, clammy, etc.

Determining Color

10 Look for apparent skin color changes that may be described as extremely pale, ashen (grey), red, blue, yellowish or black-and-blue blotches.

11 If the patient has dark skin, check for color changes on the nail beds, lips, gums, tongue, palms, whites of the eyes and ear lobes.

SAMPLE – Allergies

1 Ask if patient is allergic to anything – food, drugs, airborne matter, etc.

2 Has the patient ingested or taken anything he may be allergic to? Has the patient been bitten or stung by an organism?

3 Treat severe allergic reactions as a medical emergency and follow primary care procedures.

4 A severe allergic reaction (anaphylaxis) can be treated by epinephrine (adrenalin). People who have suffered a prior episode of anaphylaxis often have prescribed for them an autoinjector of epinephrine (adrenalin). Have the patient use the autoinjector or assist them with its use.

5 In unusual circumstances when advanced medical assistance is not available, a second dose of epinephrine (adrenalin) may be given if symptoms of anaphylaxis persist.

SAMPLE – Medications

1 Ask if patient takes medication for a medical condition. Questions may include:

▲ Do you take medication?

▲ If yes, what type of medication do you take?

▲ Did you take medication today?

▲ How much medication did you take and when?

2 If possible, collect all medication to give to EMS personnel and/or get name of the doctor who prescribed the medication.

SAMPLE – Preexisting Medical Conditions

1 Ask if patient has a preexisting medical condition (e.g., heart condition, diabetes, asthma, epilepsy, etc.)

SAMPLE – Last Meal

1 Ask when patient last had a meal and what patient ate. Ask if he has consumed any alcohol or recreational drugs.

SAMPLE – Events

1 Ask patient about and note events leading up to illness.

TRY IT

In your practice group, perform a primary assessment on a responsive patient. Next, begin your Illness Assessment. In this situation, EMS is either delayed or unavailable.

One person is the guide, reading the steps, one is the patient, while the other is the Emergency Responder conducting the illness assessment. By conducting an illness assessment on a healthy person in class, you will be able to recognize differences later when you assist an unhealthy person.

Make sure everyone has the chance to act as the Emergency Responder. Alter circumstances as directed by your instructor.

Secondary Care Skill 3
Bandaging

Your Goal

Demonstrate how to bandage a foot, leg, hand or arm using roller bandages and triangular bandages.

How It's Done

1 Put on gloves.

2 Apply bandage directly over a sterile dressing covering the wound.

3 Apply bandage below wound and work upward toward the heart.

4 Wrap roller bandage firmly and consistently – avoid making bandage too loose or too tight.

5 Secure end of bandage by tying, tucking or taping it in place.

Key Points

◆ Use this skill to determine what first aid may be needed in the event of any injury – especially if EMS is either delayed or unavailable.

◆ Remember to stop, think, then act – assess scene and alert EMS if necessary.

◆ Protect yourself and your patient from disease transmission by using barriers if available. Do not delay emergency care if barriers are not available.

◆ Perform a patient responsiveness check by giving the Responder Statement, and if no response, tap patient on collarbone.

◆ Perform a primary assessment and use the *Cycle of Care* to continually monitor a patient's medical status.

◆ Perform an injury assessment.

◆ A first aid kit may include several different types of bandages including triangular bandages, adhesive strips, conforming bandages, gauze rollers (nonelastic cotton) and elastic rollers.

◆ Choose the best bandage based on the injury or make the best use of whatever is available.

Secure Bandage

Avoid Making Bandage Too Tight

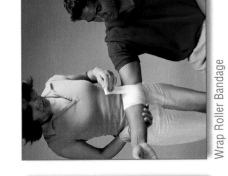

Wrap Roller Bandage

Cover Wound

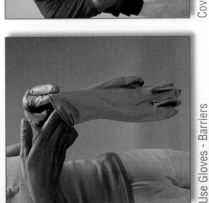

Use Gloves - Barriers

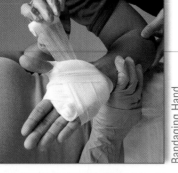

Bandaging Hand

Proper Placement

Supporting Possible Broken Ribs

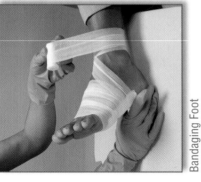

Bandaging Foot

Support Injury with Triangular Bandage

Secure Bandage - Tie End

6   When bandaging the foot, secure bandage by wrapping it around the ankle several times then back over injury site on the foot.

7   When bandaging hand, secure bandage by wrapping it over the thumb and around the wrist.

8   If elbow is involved, bandage below and above the joint to stabilize injury site.

9   If the knee is involved, bandage below and above the joint to stabilize the injury.

10   If there is an impaled object, bandage the object in place and do not remove.

Using Triangular Bandages

1   Use triangular bandages to support injuries of the upper arm, ribs or shoulder.

2   Place top of the triangular bandage over the shoulder.

3   Bend arm at the elbow, bring forearm across the chest and over the bandage.

4   Bring lower end of the bandage over the opposite shoulder and tie off at the back of the neck.

5   Tie off triangular bandage at the patient's elbow, locking the arm in the sling.

6   When broken ribs are suspected, use a second triangular bandage to hold the arm against the injured side of the chest. Simply tie bandage over the sling and around the chest.

TRY IT

In your practice group, practice bandaging a leg or arm using a roller bandage, then use a triangular bandage to make an arm sling. Vary the wound sites – your instructor will direct you. Remember, you only bandage wounds if EMS is either delayed or unavailable.

One person is the guide, reading the steps, one is the patient, while the other is the Emergency Responder. Make sure everyone has the chance to act as the Emergency Responder. Alter circumstances as directed by your instructor.

Secondary Care Skill 4
Splinting for Dislocations and Fractures

Your Goal

Demonstrate how to apply a splint to a dislocation or fracture.

Key Points

♦ Use this skill to determine what first aid may be needed in the event of any injury – especially if EMS is either delayed or unavailable.

♦ Remember to stop, think, then act – assess scene and alert EMS if necessary.

♦ Protect yourself and your patient from disease transmission by using barriers if available. Do not delay emergency care if barriers are not available.

♦ Perform a patient responsiveness check by giving the Responder Statement, and if no response, tap patient on collarbone.

♦ Perform a primary assessment and use the *Cycle of Care* to continually monitor a patient's medical status.

♦ Perform an injury assessment.

♦ Use splinting to protect and immobilize a fractured, dislocated, sprained or strained body part.

♦ Splints may include a variety of rigid devices including commercial splints or improvised splints (rolled newspapers or magazines, heavy cardboard, padded board, etc.). You may also secure the injured part to an uninjured body part (e.g., injured finger to an uninjured finger; injured arm to the chest, etc.).

♦ Splint the injury in the position found. Do not try to straighten. Try to minimize movement of the extremity until you complete splinting.

♦ If available, place splint materials on both sides of the injury site. This prevents rotation of the injured extremity and prevents the bones from touching if two or more bones are involved.

♦ Splint only if you can do so without causing more discomfort and pain to the patient.

Pad Splint

Check Circulation

Place Arm in Sling

Choose Correct Splint

Bandage Splint in Place

How It's Done

1 Choose a splint long enough to immobilize joints above and below the injury.

2 When using rigid splints, apply ample padding between splint and the injury. Add padding to the natural body hollows as well.

3 Bandage splint in place by using a roller bandage, a triangular bandage, an elastic bandage, adhesive tape or other available materials.

4 Always check circulation before and after splinting. If pulse is absent, loosen the splint until the pulse returns. To do this, look for color of tissue in fingernails and toenails.

5 If the fracture is in the upper arm, place arm in sling after splinting.

 **TRY IT**

In your practice group, practice splinting a leg or arm. Try a variety of instructor-supplied splinting material. Be resourceful and use possible splinting material found around you.

One person is the guide, reading the steps, one is the patient, while the other is the Emergency Responder. Make sure everyone has the chance to act as the Emergency Responder. Alter circumstances as directed by your instructor.

Section THREE

Emergency REFERENCE

Contents

Alphabetical Order

EFR Reference

This section gives you important information on specific emergency care situations – what the medical emergency is, ways to identify it via signs and symptoms, and how to treat it.

Assembling a First Aid Kit

Build a well-stocked first aid kit:

(Suggested items – specialized items may be necessary based on regional first aid needs.)

▲ Durable noncorrosive case
▲ *Emergency First Response Participant Manual* and *Care at a Glance* – used as reference.
▲ Emergency phone numbers/coins/phone card – used in an emergency to assist with remembering important contact information
▲ Gloves – to protect rescuer against bloodborne pathogens
▲ Ventilation barriers – to protect rescuer against disease transmission
▲ Large absorbent dressings; various sizes – to help stop bleeding
▲ Sterile gauze pads; various sizes – to help stop bleeding and dress wounds
▲ Clinging rolled bandages; various sizes – to dress wounds
▲ Adhesive bandages; various sizes – to dress wounds
▲ Adhesive tape – to dress wounds
▲ Nonadherent, dry pads – to dress burn wounds
▲ Triangular bandages – to immobilize dislocations and fractures
▲ Sterile cotton – to dress wounds
▲ Cotton tipped swabs – to clean wounds
▲ Bandage scissors – to cut bandages and patient's clothes
▲ Tongue depressors – to check vital signs during illness assessment; could also be used as splinting material for finger dislocations and fractures
▲ Tweezers – to assist in removing foreign material
▲ Needle – to assist in removing foreign material
▲ Safety pins – to attach and secure bandages
▲ Penlight – for light and to use as an examination tool
▲ Oral thermometer – to measure temperature as a vital sign
▲ Squeeze bottle of water – for hydration and patients with heat stroke; burns, eye or wound wash

Protect Yourself and Others

Where possible (for maximum protection), when attending to an injured or ill patient:

◆ Use gloves.
◆ Use ventilation masks or shields when providing CPR.
◆ Use eye or face shields; including eyeglasses or sunglasses, goggles and face masks when assisting a patient who is bleeding.
◆ Always wash your hands or any other area exposed to body fluids with antibacterial soap and water. Scrub vigorously, creating lots of lather. If water is not available, use antibacterial wipes or cleansing liquids.

▲ Splints – to immobilize dislocations and fractures
▲ Emergency blanket – for warmth; to cover patients with shock
▲ Cold packs – for bruises, strains, sprains, eye injuries, stings and dislocations and fractures
▲ Hot packs – for venomous bites and stings
▲ Vinegar – to neutralize stinging cells of jellyfish
▲ Plastic bags – use to dispose of gloves and medical waste; may be used in lieu of actual gloves as a barrier
▲ Small paper cups – for drinking and to cover eye injuries
▲ Denatured alcohol – for disinfectant, not to be used on wounds
▲ Antibacterial soap – to clean wounds
▲ Antiseptic solution or wipes – for wounds
▲ Antibiotic ointment – for wounds
▲ Hydrocortisone ointment – for stings or irritations
▲ Aspirin and nonaspirin pain relievers – to reduce swelling and patient discomfort
▲ Antihistamine tablets – for allergic reactions
▲ Sugar packets, candy or fruit juice – for low blood sugar patients
▲ Activated charcoal – for poisoning

Primary Care

Adult CPR

1 **STOP** – Assess and observe scene.
2 **THINK** – Consider your safety and form action plan.
3 **ACT** – Check responsiveness.
4 **ALERT** EMS.
5 Is the patient's **AIRWAY** open? Is he **BREATHING** normally?
6 *Not breathing normally* – Call EMS and locate an AED; position patient on back and remove obvious obstructions from mouth.
7 Perform 30 **CHEST COMPRESSIONS** by pushing hard and fast at a rate of 100 compressions per minute.
8 Place ventilation barrier over patient's mouth and/or nose. Pinch patient's nose closed.
9 Give two rescue **BREATHS, each lasting about one second. Deliver breaths with enough air to make the patient's chest rise.**
10 Continue with cycles of 30 compressions and two rescue breaths.
11 **DEFIBRILLATION** by EMS or Automated External Defibrillator (AED) as soon as possible.
12 If the patient begins breathing, manage Serious bleeding, Shock and Spinal injury.

Infant and Child CPR (0 – 8 years old)

For infants and children, rescuers should make the following modifications to adult CPR:

▲ If you are on your own, perform CPR for two minutes (ERC - one minute) before going for help.
▲ Compress the chest by approximately one-third of its depth. Use two fingers for infant or use one or two hands (as with adults) for child over 1 year.

Choking Adult

NOTE – Different procedures for choking come from the American Heart Association (AHA - used in North, South and Central America), European Resuscitation Council (ERC), plus Australian and New Zealand Resuscitation Council (ARC/NZRC). ERC: Use back blows and abdominal thrusts for conscious choking patients and chest thrusts for obese or pregnant choking patients. North, South and Central America: Use abdominal thrusts for conscious patients and chest thrusts for obese or pregnant choking patients. ARC/NZRC: Use up to five back blows and chest thrusts for conscious choking patients.

1 **STOP** – Assess and observe scene.
2 **THINK** – Consider your safety and form action plan.
3 **ACT** – Check responsiveness. Patient is conscious, grasping throat, is not breathing, and cannot make noise. Perform Back Blows, Abdominal Thrusts or Chest Thrusts as per guidelines in your local area.

Deliver up to five forceful **BACK BLOWS** by striking the child between the shoulder blades with the heel of your other hand.

If these five back blows do not dislodge the object, give up to five **ABDOMINAL THRUSTS** or **CHEST THRUSTS** as per guidelines in your region.

To perform abdominal thrusts, stand or kneel behind the child and place your arms around the upper abdomen. Then, make a fist with the thumb side above the navel but below the breastbone. Cover your fist with your other hand.

Perform five, quick inward and upward thrusts. Each thrust is a separate, distinct movement.

Continue to give a combination of five back blows and five abdominal thrusts until the object is forced out, the child can breathe, speak or cough forcefully or the child becomes unconscious.

If the child becomes unconscious, begin **CPR**. If alone, give CPR for five cycles, 30 compressions and two breaths, then call EMS.

Children who receive emergency care for choking must receive medical evaluation to rule out any life-threatening complications.

Choking Infant

1 **STOP** – Is the infant choking?
2 **THINK** – Is the airway completely or severely blocked?
3 **ACT** – Send someone to **ALERT** EMS.

▲ Place infant's stomach on your forearm. Support infant's head by placing jaw on your fingers.

▲ With infant's head slightly lower than the body, deliver five forceful **BACK BLOWS** between shoulder blades with heel of your hand.

▲ If object is not dislodged, support infant's head while keeping spine straight and turn infant over.

▲ Locate chest thrust compression site. (Draw a line from nipple to nipple and place your index finger on the line in middle of chest. Place two fingers just below the line. Lift your index finger.)

▲ With infant's head lower than body, provide five **CHEST THRUSTS**. Continue

▲ If object is not dislodged, repeat back blows and chest thrusts. Continue until object is dislodged or infant becomes unresponsive.

▲ If infant becomes unresponsive, begin **CPR**. If you are alone, provide the infant two minutes of CPR then alert EMS. Once EMS is alerted, continue emergency care.

---

4 **Ask patient** – *Are you Choking?* **Yes – Alert EMS, Give Emergency Care.**
5 **Emergency Care**
  Give Patient Five Up To Back Blows.

▲ Take a position to the side and slightly behind the patient.

▲ Support the chest with one hand, and lean the patient forward.

▲ Firmly strike patient between shoulder blades with heel of hand, five times.

▲ Still choking? Give abdominal thrusts OR chest thrusts.

▲ Patient becomes unconscious – Give CPR.

6 **Emergency Care**
  Give Patient Up To Five Abdominal Thrusts.

▲ Stand behind the patient and place your arms around waist.

▲ Locate patient's navel – thrust site is just above navel.

▲ Make a fist and place the thumb side on the thrust site.

▲ Place your other hand over the outside of the fist.

▲ Bend your arms and elbows outward to avoid squeezing the rib cage.

▲ Perform five quick inward and upward thrusts.

▲ Still choking? Give back blows OR chest thrusts.

▲ Patient becomes unconscious – Give CPR.

7 **Emergency Care**
  Give Patient Up To Five Chest Thrusts.

▲ Stand behind the patient and place your arms around the body, under armpits.

▲ Make fist, placing thumb side on thrust site – between nipples.

▲ Place the other hand over the outside of the fist.

▲ Perform five quick inward thrusts until the object is expelled or the patient becomes unconscious.

▲ Avoid putting pressure on the rib cage.

▲ Still Choking? Give back blows OR abdominal thrusts.

▲ Patient Becomes Unconscious – Give CPR.

Choking Child

1 **STOP** – Ask the child *"are you choking?"*
2 **THINK** – Is the airway completely or severely blocked?
3 **ACT** – Send someone to **ALERT** EMS.

▲ Take a position slightly behind the child.

▲ Provide support by placing one arm diagonally across the chest and lean the child forward.

Injury First Aid

Injury Assessment

1 **STOP** – Assess and observe scene.
2 **THINK** – Consider your safety and form action plan.
3 **ACT** – Check responsiveness and **ALERT** EMS.
4 **Perform a primary assessment and monitor patient using the** *Cycle of Care.*
5 **Explain Assessment Procedure to Patient – Wear Gloves**
6 **Begin At Patient's Head**

▲ Treat patient in position found.
▲ Stabilize head/neck – ask patient to respond verbally.
▲ Check forehead, cheeks, chin for deformities.
▲ Check ears, nose for blood/fluid.
▲ Ask patient to track (with eyes only, no head movement) your finger in front of the eyes – check for smooth tracking.
▲ Check pupils – size, equal or unequal, and reaction to light.
▲ Feel skull/neck for abnormalities.

7 **Shoulders, Arms, Chest, Abdomen**

▲ Slide your hands over shoulder blades and gently push your palms against the back.
▲ Move your hands outward to shoulders and gently press inward.
▲ Run two fingers cautiously over collarbones.
▲ Slide hand down each arm – stabilizing joints (shoulder, elbow, wrist).
  ◆ Check for swelling, hardness, tissue softness, points of tenderness or deformities.
  ◆ Ask patient to wiggle fingers, squeeze.
▲ Gently press rib cage.
▲ Reach around and feel along spinal column from each side without moving patient.
▲ Gently push on abdomen – right/left side, above and below navel.

8 **Hips, Legs, Feet**

▲ Feel the hipbones gently; do not push inward.
▲ Slide hand down each leg, knee, lower leg, ankle.
  ◆ Check for swelling, hardness, tissue softness, points of tenderness or deformities.
  ◆ Ask patient to wiggle toes, press sole of foot against your hand.

9 **Note areas of pain or abnormality to report to EMS personnel.**
10 **Continue to monitor patient using the** *Cycle of Care.*
11 **Avoid giving injured patient anything to eat or drink should they need surgery.**

Dislocations and Fractures

Out-of-socket joints, cracked, broken, separated and shattered bones.

Important Information

▲ *Dislocations occur when a great deal of pressure is placed on a joint. The patient's joint appears deformed and the injury is very painful.*
▲ *Suspect a fracture if, after a fall or blow, a limb appears to be in an unnatural position, is unusable, swells or bruises rapidly or is extremely painful at a specific point.*
▲ *Only splint an injury if EMS care or transport to a medical facility is delayed and if you can do so without causing more discomfort and pain to patient.*
▲ *All dislocations and fractures need professional medical attention.*

Patient Care

1 **STOP** – Assess and observe scene.
2 **THINK** – Consider your safety and form action plan.
3 **ACT** – Check responsiveness and **ALERT** EMS, as appropriate.
4 For patient involved in a major fall, collision or blow, conduct injury assessment to determine extent of all injuries besides obvious dislocation or fracture.
5 If EMS is delayed or unavailable, prepare patient for transport. Choose a splint that is long enough to immobilize the bones above and below the unstable joint.
6 Splint injury in position found. Do not try to straighten. Minimize movement while splinting.
7 Bandage splint in place by using a triangle bandage or other available materials.
8 Fractured fingers and toes may be taped to adjacent fingers or toes for support.
9 Check circulation before and after splinting. Loosen splint if it interferes with circulation.
10 For closed fractures or dislocation, apply cold compress to area during transport to reduce swelling.

Minor Cuts, Scrapes and Bruises

Non life-threatening wounds – lacerations, scratches, abrasions, gashes, punctures and bumps.

Important Information

▲ Deep cuts or puncture, wounds with embedded objects, human or animal bites that penetrate or old infected wounds need to be treated by a medical professional.

▲ Patients with wounds that do not stop bleeding with direct pressure or pressure points need immediate EMS care.

Patient Care – Cuts and Scrapes

1 Wear gloves and other barriers to protect yourself and patient from disease transmission.

2 If necessary, control bleeding with direct pressure.

3 Thoroughly wash wound with water to remove all dirt and particles.

4 Cover wound with a nonadhesive dressing and bandage securely.

5 Check wound daily for signs of infection – redness, tenderness or presence of pus (yellowish or greenish fluid at wound site).

Patient Care – Bruises

1 Apply cold compress to injured area as soon as possible.

2 Elevate affected area, if possible.

Dental Injury

Fractured jaw, loose tooth, broken tooth, dislodged tooth, bitten lip or tongue.

Important Information

▲ Treat dental injuries resulting from trauma to the head, neck, face or mouth as medical emergencies. Follow primary and secondary care procedures.

▲ Send patient to a dentist for treatment when dental injuries are due to wear and tear, or minor mishaps. Provide secondary care.

Patient Care – Dislodged Tooth

1 Wear gloves to protect yourself and patient from disease transmission.

2 Locate dislodged tooth. Do not touch the root.

3 Hold tooth by crown and rinse gently with saline solution, milk or water.

4 Keep tooth moist in saline solution, milk or water while transporting to dentist.

5 If unable to get to dentist within 60 minutes, reimplant tooth into socket as soon as possible. Teeth reimplanted within 30 to 60 minutes have a good chance of reattaching to socket.

6 Encourage patient to follow up with continued dental care.

Strains and Sprains

Injured, stretched or torn muscles, tendons and ligaments

Important Information

▲ General treatment involves RICE – Rest, Ice, Compression and Elevation for the first 72 hours after injury.

▲ Patients should consult a medical professional to determine the extent of the injury and to ensure no bones are broken.

Patient Care

1 **REST** – take stress off injured area and avoid use as much as possible.

2 **ICE** – apply cold compress to injured area for up to 20 minutes. Repeat icing at least four times a day.

3 **COMPRESSION** – wrap area with elastic bandage.

4 **ELEVATE** – raise injured area above the heart as much as possible.

5 If patient must use injured area, tape or splint to provide stability and prevent further injury.

6 Anti-inflammatory tablets or pain relievers may reduce pain and inflammation.

7 Encourage patient to follow up with a doctor.

Eye Injuries

Cuts, penetrations, blows, chemical splashes and irritants.

Important Information

▲ All eye injuries are potentially serious due to risk to patient's vision.

▲ Treat eye injuries that result from trauma to the head or face as medical emergencies. Follow primary and secondary care procedures.

▲ Never apply pressure to the eye and be careful not to rub it.

▲ If patient wears contact lenses, remove them only if it will not cause further damage to the eye.

▲ *Encourage patients with any eye soreness or irritation to see an eye specialist for treatment as soon as possible. Provide secondary care.*

▲ *Encourage patient to keep calm. Increased activity and blood pressure can cause important eye fluids to leak causing further harm to the eye.*

▲ *Do not touch or try to remove an object embedded in the eye. Do not touch anything that is sticking to the colored part of the eye.*

Patient Care – Cuts and Penetrations to Eye

1 **STOP** – Assess and observe scene.
2 **THINK** – Consider your safety and form action plan.
3 **ACT** – Check responsiveness and **ALERT** EMS.
4 Perform a primary assessment and monitor patient using the *Cycle of Care.*
5 Apply a sterile dressing and lightly bandage the eye.
6 If penetrating object protrudes from eye, place a small paper cup over eye and bandage in place. Do NOT remove object.
7 Consider covering both eyes to deter patient from moving injured eye.
8 Continue to monitor patient using the *Cycle of Care* until EMS arrives.

Patient Care – Blow to Eye

1 **STOP** – Assess and observe scene.
2 **THINK** – Consider your safety and form action plan.
3 **ACT** – Check responsiveness and **ALERT** EMS, as appropriate.
4 Perform a primary assessment and monitor patient using the *Cycle of Care.*
5 Apply cold compresses for 15 minutes.
6 If EMS is not called, encourage patient to see eye specialist as soon as possible.

Patient Care – Chemical Splashes in the Eye

1 **STOP** – Assess and observe scene.
2 **THINK** – Consider your safety and form action plan.
3 **ACT** – Check responsiveness and **ALERT** EMS, as appropriate.
4 Monitor patient using the *Cycle of Care.*
5 Immediately flush eye with water until EMS arrives or for a minimum of 15 minutes.
6 Open eye as wide as possible and ask patient to roll eye to aid flushing.

7 Be careful that the rinsing water does not splash into the uninjured eye or yourself. Ask the patient to hold a sterile, non-fluffy dressing over the eye. Lightly bandage dressing in place if EMS will be delayed or the patient will be sent to hospital. Identify the chemical if possible.

Patient Care – Irritants in the Eye

1 Wear gloves to protect yourself and patient from disease transmission.
2 Inspect eye and attempt to locate irritant.
3 Either you or the patient should lift the upper lid and gently pull it down over lower eye lashes.
4 Encourage patient to blink and let tears wash irritant away.
5 If irritant remains, flush the eye with a gentle stream of water.
6 If irritant remains, carefully attempt to dislodge it with a sterile moistened cloth.
7 If irritant remains, have patient seek treatment from an eye specialist.

Electrical Injury

Electric shock, electrocution and electrical burns

Important Information

▲ *Any contact with electricity can cause life-threatening injuries such as cardiopulmonary arrest, deep burns and internal tissue damage.*

▲ *Treat electrical shock that alters the patient's consciousness, results in burns or is associated with collisions or falls as medical emergencies. Follow primary and secondary care procedures.*

▲ *Any injury caused by electric shock should be examined by a medical professional.*

Patient Care

1 **STOP** – Assess and observe scene – *Is patient still in contact with electricity?*
2 **THINK** – Consider your safety and form action plan – *Make sure electricity is off.*
3 **ACT** – Check responsiveness and **ALERT** EMS, as appropriate.
4 Perform a primary assessment
5 Monitor patient using the *Cycle of Care.*
6 If patient is responsive, perform a secondary assessment – look for burns.
7 Treat burns by flushing with cool water until EMS arrives. (See *Burns* for more information)
8 If EMS is not called, encourage patient to see a doctor.

Temperature-Related Injuries

Burns

Thermal, chemical and electrical burns.

Important Information

▶ First-degree burns affect only the outer skin layer. The skin is red, slightly swollen and painful to touch. Sunburn usually falls into this category.

▶ Second-degree burns go into the second skin layer and appear as blisters on red, splotchy skin.

▶ Third-degree burns involve all layers of the skin – even underlying tissue. These serious burns are often painless due to nerve destruction. They appear as charred black or dry and white areas.

▶ Treat any large burn on the face, hands, feet, groin, buttocks or a major joint as a medical emergency. Follow primary and secondary care procedures.

▶ Never put ice, butter, grease, ointments, creams or oils on a burn.

▶ Do not peel off any clothes or break any blisters.

▶ Do not burst any blisters.

▶ Do not use fluffy materials – example: cotton wool, which will stick to the burned area.

▶ Where possible, elevate burnt limbs.

▶ Patients with third-degree burns; second-degree burns that cover more than 1% body surface area; first degree burns that cover over 5% body surface area; burns to the hands, feet, face or genitals, mixed degree burns, burns extending around a limb or burns on children, should go to hospital.

▶ Patients with second degree burns must see a doctor.

Patient Care – Major Burns

1 **STOP** – Assess and observe scene – Where is the heat source?

2 **THINK** – Consider your safety and form action plan – Is patient's clothing or surroundings still on fire or hot?

3 **ACT** – Check responsiveness and **ALERT** EMS.

4 Perform a primary assessment and monitor patient using the Cycle of Care.

5 If patient is responsive, perform secondary assessment to determine extent of burns.

6 Help the patient lie down, but ensure burnt area does not come into contact with ground.

7 Douse the burnt area with cold liquid for at least 10 minutes. Continue cooling the area until pain is relieved.

8 Carefully remove clothing from around the burnt area and remove any constricting items, such as watches, belts etc before swelling begins.

9 Cover burns with a sterile dressing or other non-fluffy material available (e.g. sheet, triangular bandage). Cling film could also be used if applied lengthways.

10 For finger or toe burns, remove jewelry and separate with dry, sterile dressings.

11 For burns to the airway, loosen clothing around the neck, offer ice or small sips of cold water.

12 Continue to monitor patient using the Cycle of Care until EMS arrives – manage shock.

13 If trained, provide oxygen to patients with a major burn injury.

14 Monitor and record vital signs.

Patient Care – Minor Burns
(first degree and small second-degree)

1 Wear gloves to protect yourself and patient from disease transmission.

2 Flush or soak burn in cool water for at least ten minutes. If possible, remove any jewelry, watches, belts or constricting items from the injured area before it begins to swell.

3 Cover area with a sterile (non-fluffy) dressing and bandage loosely.

4 Check burn daily for signs of infection – redness, tenderness or presence of pus (yellowish or greenish fluid at wound site).

Patient Care – Chemical Burn

1 **STOP** – Assess and observe scene – What and where are chemicals?

2 **THINK** – Consider your safety and form action plan – How can you avoid chemical contact?

3 **ACT** – Check responsiveness and **ALERT** EMS, as appropriate.

4 Perform a primary assessment and monitor patient using the Cycle of Care.

5 For liquid chemicals, flush skin surface with cool, running water for at least 20 minutes.

6 For powder chemicals, brush off skin before flushing with water.

7 Cover burn with a dry, sterile dressing or a clean cloth.

8 If EMS is not called, encourage patient to see a doctor.

Hypothermia

Severe hypothermia – body temperature below 32° C/90° F
Mild hypothermia – body temperature lowered to 34° C/93° F

Important Information

▲ *A patient suffering from severe hypothermia may be disoriented, confused, uncoordinated or completely unresponsive.*

▲ *A patient suffering from mild hypothermia may be conscious and alert, yet shivering and displaying slightly impaired coordination.*

▲ *Treat hypothermia that alters the patient's consciousness or impairs coordination as a medical emergency. Follow primary care procedures.*

▲ *A severely hypothermic patient may be breathing or have a pulse at such a low rate and intensity that it is difficult to detect. Therefore, resuscitation attempts should never be abandoned until the patient has been rewarmed.*

Patient Care – Severe Hypothermia

1 **STOP** – Assess and observe scene – *Has patient been exposed to a cold environment?*

2 **THINK** – Consider your safety and form action plan – *Is a warm, dry area nearby?*

3 **ACT** – Check responsiveness and **ALERT** EMS.

4 Perform a primary assessment and monitor patient using the *Cycle of Care.*

5 Do not move patient unless necessary to prevent further heat loss. Handling may cause irregular heartbeat.

6 Remove wet clothing without jostling patient. Cover patient with warm blankets or thick clothing.

7 Continue to monitor patient using the *Cycle of Care* until EMS arrives. Monitor and record vital signs.

Patient Care – Mild Hypothermia

1 Move patient to a warm and dry sheltered area and wrap in warm blankets or clothes.

2 If patient is wet, provide with dry clothing.

3 Give warm, nonalcoholic, noncaffeinated drinks.

4 Continue to support patient until completely rewarmed. Monitor and record vital signs.

Frostbite

Frostnip, superficial and deep frostbite

Important Information

▲ *Frostbite occurs when an area of the body freezes and ice crystals form within cells.*

▲ *Frostnip is the first stage that affects the surface skin. The skin becomes red, painful and may itch.*

▲ *Superficial frostbite affects skin layers, but not the soft tissue below. The skin becomes hard and white.*

▲ *Deep frostbite affects entire tissue layers including muscles, tendons, blood vessels, and nerves. The area may be white, deep purple or red with blisters, and feel hard and woody.*

▲ *Treat frostbite as a medical emergency. Follow primary and secondary care procedures.*

Patient Care

1 **STOP** – Assess and observe scene – *Has patient been exposed to a cold environment?*

2 **THINK** – Consider your safety and form action plan – *Is a warm, dry area nearby?*

3 **ACT** – Check responsiveness and **ALERT** EMS.

4 Perform a primary and secondary assessment. Monitor patient using the *Cycle of Care.*

5 Move patient to a warm and dry sheltered area. Remove any constricting items such as jewelry.

6 Begin to warm affected areas with your body heat or by immersing in warm (not hot) water. Rescuer should check the water to make sure it is only warm. Warm slowly.

7 Do not rub or massage frostbitten areas. Note that rewarming may be very painful.

8 Continue to monitor patient using the *Cycle of Care* until EMS arrives.

Illness First Aid

Heat Stroke and Exhaustion

Heat stroke – body temperature higher than 40°C/104°F
Heat exhaustion – fluid loss and body temperature up to 40°C/104°F

Important Information

▲ *Heat stroke occurs when the body's temperature control system fails and body temperature rises dangerously high. It is a life-threatening condition.*

▲ *Patients with heat stroke may have hot, dry, flushed skin, rapid pulse and be disoriented, confused or unconscious.*

▲ *Treat heat stroke as a medical emergency. Follow primary care procedures.*

▲ *Heat exhaustion occurs when fluid intake does not compensate for perspiration loss.*

▲ *Patients with heat exhaustion may have cool and clammy skin, weak pulse and complain of nausea, dizziness, weakness and anxiety.*

Patient Care – Heat Stroke

1 **STOP** – Assess and observe scene – *Has patient been exposed to a hot environment?*

2 **THINK** – Consider your safety and form action plan – *Is a cool, shady area nearby?*

3 **ACT** – Check responsiveness and **ALERT** EMS.

4 Perform a primary assessment. Monitor patient using the *Cycle of Care.*

5 Move patient to a cool, shady area.

6 Immediately cool patient by spraying or sponging with cool water.

7 Cover patient with wet cloth and continue to monitor patient using the *Cycle of Care* until EMS arrives.

8 Replace wet cloth with dry one if temperature returns to normal.

Patient Care – Heat Exhaustion

1 Move patient to cool location.

2 Urge patient to lie down and elevate legs.

3 Provide patient with cool water or an electrolyte-containing beverage to drink every few minutes.

4 Cool patient by misting with water and fanning.

5 Continue to support patient until completely cooled.

6 If EMS is not called, encourage patient to see a doctor.

7 If condition deteriorates, place patient in recovery position and activate EMS.

Illness Assessment

Illness Assessment – An illness is an *unhealthy condition of the body.* An illness assessment helps you identify and report medical problems that affect a patient's health and may aid in the patient's treatment.

Important Information

▲ *Use this skill to determine what first aid may be needed in the event that Emergency Medical Service is either delayed or unavailable.*

▲ *Only perform illness assessments on conscious, responsive patients.*

▲ *When giving information to EMS personnel, avoid using the word normal. Provide measured rates per minute and descriptive terminology.*

Patient Care

1 **STOP** – Assess and observe scene.

2 **THINK** – Consider your safety and form action plan.

3 **ACT** – Check responsiveness.

4 **ALERT** EMS.

▲ Find a paper and a pen/pencil to record illness assessment information. Use Illness Assessment Record Sheet at the end of this section.

▲ If possible, have someone else record information.

▲ Put on gloves.

Illness Assessment *(continued)*

S.A.M.P.L.E. – Signs and Symptoms

▲ How does patient feel now?
▲ Determine patient's pulse rate (use carotid or radial pulse; count beats for 30 seconds, multiply by two).
▲ Describe patient's pulse: rapid, strong, weak, slow?
▲ Determine patient's respiration rate.
▲ Patient's breathing is: rapid, slow, labored, wheezing, gasping?
▲ Patient complains of: shortness of breath, dizziness/lightheadedness, chest pain, numbness, tingling in arms/legs?
▲ Patient's skin is: warm, hot, cool, clammy, wet, very dry?
▲ Color of patient's skin under the lip is: pale, ashen, red, blue, yellowish, black and blue blotches?

Finding Pulse Rate

◆ To find pulse rate using the carotid artery:
↑ Locate the patient's Adam's apple with the index and middle fingers of one hand.
↑ Slide the fingers down into the groove of the neck on the side closest to you.
↑ If you can't find the pulse on the side closest to you, move to the opposite side.
↑ Never try to feel the carotid pulse on both sides at the same time.
↑ Count the number of beats in 30 seconds and multiply by two to determine the heartbeats per minute.

◆ To find pulse rate using the radial artery:
↑ Locate artery on patient's wrist, thumb side of hand.
↑ Slide two or three fingers into the groove of the wrist immediately below hand on the thumb side.
↑ Do not use your thumb when taking a radial pulse.
↑ Count the number of beats in 30 seconds and multiply by two to determine the heartbeats per minute.

◆ Determine whether the pulse may be described as rapid, strong or weak.

Checking Respiration

◆ Look for signs and symptoms of respiratory distress, including:
↑ Wheezing, gurgling or high-pitched noises when the patient breathes.
↑ Patient complains of shortness of breath or feeling dizzy or lightheaded.
↑ Patient complains of pain in the chest and numbness or tingling in arms or legs.

◆ Evaluate breathing by either:
↑ Placing a hand on patient's abdomen or watch chest rise and fall.
↑ Counting patient's respiration for 30 seconds and multiplying by two to determine respiratory rate.

◆ Determine whether respiration may be described as fast, slow, labored, wheezing or gasping.

Checking temperature and moisture

◆ Feel patient's forehead or cheek with the back of your hand. Compare with your own temperature using your other hand on your forehead. Verify if the patient has perhaps been doing physical exercise. Determine whether the skin is warm, hot, cool, moist, clammy, etc.

Determining Color

◆ Look for apparent skin color changes under a patient's lip that may be described as extremely pale, ashen (grey), red, blue, yellowish or black-and-blue blotches.

◆ If the patient has dark skin, check for color changes on the nail beds, lips, gums, tongue, palms, whites of the eyes, and ear lobes.

Keep It Safe – Dos and Don'ts (continued)

DO NOT mix household cleaning products or other chemicals together.
DO NOT use food containers to store chemical products.
DO NOT call medicine candy.
DO NOT take medications in the dark.
DO NOT eat wild mushrooms or plant leaves, stems, roots or berries unless you are positive they are nontoxic.
DO NOT eat foods that may be spoiled or prepared in unclean conditions.

Patient Care – Ingested Poison

1 **STOP** – Assess and observe scene – *Is there a poisonous substance nearby?*
2 **THINK** – Consider your safety and form action plan – *Can the substance harm me?*
3 **ACT** – Check responsiveness and **ALERT** EMS.
4 Perform a primary assessment and monitor patient using the *Cycle of Care*.
5 For a responsive patient, conduct an illness assessment – gather information about what, when and how much poison was ingested while waiting for EMS to arrive.
6 If available, read label on substance for poisoning instructions and call Poison Control Center for direction.
7 If instructed to induce vomiting, use substance recommended by local Poison Control Center. Save vomitus and gather poison container for EMS personnel.
8 Continue to follow Poison Control Center directions and support patient until EMS arrives.

Patient Care – Inhaled Poison

1 **STOP** – Assess and observe scene – *Is there a poisonous substance or fumes nearby?* Be very cautious of entering enclosed spaces. Remember, some poisonous gases are both odorless and colorless. Emergency Responder safety must be considered at all times. You may have to wait for EMS to arrive with independent breathing equipment to assist the patient.
2 **THINK** – Consider your safety and form action plan – *Can the substance harm me?*
3 **ACT** – Check responsiveness and **ALERT** EMS.
4 If necessary, move patient to area with fresh air.
5 Perform a primary assessment and monitor patient using the *Cycle of Care*.

6 For a responsive patient, help loosen clothing around the neck and chest for easier breathing. Conduct an illness assessment – gather information about what, when and how much poison was inhaled while waiting for EMS to arrive.
7 Contact local Poison Control Center for direction. If available and permitted, administer emergency oxygen.
8 Continue to support patient until EMS arrives.

Patient Care – Absorbed Poison

1 **STOP** – Assess and observe scene – *Has patient come in contact with a poisonous substance?*
2 **THINK** – Consider your safety and form action plan – *Can the substance harm me?*
3 **ACT** – Check responsiveness and **ALERT** EMS, as appropriate.
4 Conduct an illness assessment – gather information about what, when and how much contact the patient had with poison.
5 Carefully remove contaminated clothing and brush off any poison remaining on skin.
6 Flush area with fresh water and wash skin with soap. Do not allow contaminated water to touch you or the patient.
7 For caustic chemical substances or if patient experiences severe symptoms, contact local Poison Control Center for direction.
8 If EMS is not called, encourage patient to see a doctor. Cold compresses may relieve itching.

Patient Care – Food Poisoning

1 **STOP** – Assess and observe scene – *Could the patient have eaten something spoiled, contaminated or harmful?*
2 **THINK** – Consider your safety and form action plan.
3 **ACT** – Check responsiveness and **ALERT** EMS, as appropriate.
4 Conduct an illness assessment – ask what the patient ate.
5 If patient shows signs of a severe allergic reaction, treat appropriately. (See *Allergic Reactions* for more information.) Monitor patient using the *Cycle of Care* until EMS arrives.
6 If patient vomits and has diarrhea, offer fluids to prevent dehydration. Continue to support patient until recovered. Consider saving a sample of expelled body fluids for examination by medical professionals to determine the type of poison.
7 If symptoms are severe, prolonged or get worse, transport patient to a medical facility.

Venomous Bites and Stings

Snake and reptile bites, spider bites, scorpion, bee and ant stings, aquatic life injuries

Important Information

▲ Suspect a venomous bite or sting when a venomous creature is nearby or patients state that they've been bitten or stung. If possible and safe, get a good look at the creature or capture it for positive identification, however do not take time away from patient care or put yourself at risk.

▲ Reaction to venom may depend on the patient's size, current health, previous exposure, body chemistry, location of bite or sting and how much venom was injected. Some patients have severe allergic reactions to even minor bites or stings – particularly bee stings. See Allergic Reactions for treatment of anaphylaxis.

▲ Patients bitten by a venomous snake or reptile may have fang marks along with pain, swelling and skin discoloration at bite site. They may complain of weakness, nausea, difficulty breathing, speaking or swallowing, headache, blurred vision and tingling or numbness around the face or mouth. They may have a rapid pulse, fever, chills and may vomit.

▲ Patients bitten by a venomous spider may have pain, redness and/or muscle cramps or twitching, at the bite site along with abdominal pain and muscle cramps or twitching, confusion, coma and copious secretion of saliva. The patient may also complain of headaches, nausea, difficulty breathing and dizziness. Profuse sweating and extremity numbness may occur along with tingling around the mouth. Often, symptoms do not occur for more than an hour after a bite.

▲ Insect bites and stings usually result in pain, redness, itching, and swelling at bite site. Some patients may experience delayed reactions such as fever, painful joints, hives and swollen glands.

▲ Many aquatic life stings result in burning or sharp pain at the sting site along with swelling and/or red rash and welts. Some patients may experience shock, unconsciousness, respiratory difficulty or arrest, weakness, nausea and vomiting.

▲ Some bites or stings by venomous creatures result in no venom being injected into the patient and cause only minor irritation. However, because symptoms may be delayed, encourage the patient to seek professional medical follow up to prevent future disability.

▲ Treat any bite or sting by a highly venomous creature as a medical emergency. Follow primary care procedures.

▲ Treat any bite or sting that produces a deep wound, or alters the patient's breathing or consciousness level, as a medical emergency. Follow primary care procedures.

▲ If possible, contact your local Poison Control Center for directions while waiting for EMS to arrive.

▲ For many venomous bites and stings, use pressure immobilization to slow the spread of venom. Technique is pictured below.

Pressure Immobilization Bandage

Apply a broad, firm bandage over the bite as soon as possible. Keep the bitten area still.

The bandage should be as tight as you would apply to a sprained ankle.

Extend the bandages as high as possible.

Apply a splint to the limb.

Bind it firmly to as much of the limb as possible.

Patient Care – Snake Bites

1 **STOP** – Assess and observe scene – *Is there a venomous snake nearby?* Remember, some snakes may bite more than once. Protect yourself. Treat all snake bites as potentially lethal and manage as listed below.

2 **THINK** – Consider your safety and form action plan – *Can it reach me or the patient?*

3 **ACT** – Check responsiveness and **ALERT** EMS.

4 Perform a primary assessment and monitor patient using the *Cycle of Care.*

5 Once EMS is contacted, obtain and follow local medical control directions for field treatment prior to their arrival.

6 In general, keep the patient quiet by having the patient lie down and try to relax.

7 Unless directed by EMS to do otherwise, avoid cleaning the wound as saliva from the snake may assist EMS in identifying the snake.

8 If EMS is delayed or unavailable, you must transport patient. Administration of antivenin is the only effective treatment for poisonous snakebites. Therefore, prompt transport to a medical facility is important. Carry the patient if possible or have the patient walk slowly.

9 Place direct pressure on the wound with a sterile dressing, pad or gloved hand.

10 Next, apply a pressure immobilization bandage.

11 Continue to monitor patient using the *Cycle of Care* until EMS arrives or during transport.

Patient Care – Spider Bites

1 **STOP** – Assess and observe scene – *Is there a venomous insect nearby?*

2 **THINK** – Consider your safety and form action plan – *Can it reach me or the patient?*

3 **ACT** – Check responsiveness and **ALERT** EMS, as appropriate.

4 Perform a primary assessment and monitor patient using the *Cycle of Care.*

5 Once EMS is contacted, obtain and follow local medical control directions for field treatment prior to their arrival.

6 If patient shows signs of a severe allergic reaction, treat appropriately. (See *Allergic Reactions* for more information.) Monitor patient using the *Cycle of Care* until EMS arrives.

7 Reassure and keep patient still and at rest.

8 Depending on the directions from EMS: a) clean the bite area with soap and water or rubbing alcohol, b) apply cold compress to area and elevate or c) apply a pressure immobilization bandage.

9 Transport to medical facility as antivenin exists for some spiders.

Patient Care – Insect Stings (scorpion, bee, wasp and ant)

1 **STOP** – Assess and observe scene – *Is there a venomous insect nearby?*

2 **THINK** – Consider your safety and form action plan – *Can it reach me or the patient?*

3 **ACT** – Check responsiveness and **ALERT** EMS, as appropriate.

4 Perform a primary assessment and monitor patient using the *Cycle of Care.*

5 Once EMS is contacted, obtain and follow local medical control directions for field treatment prior to their arrival.

6 If patient shows signs of a severe allergic reaction, treat appropriately. (See *Allergic Reactions* for more information.) Monitor patient using the *Cycle of Care* until EMS arrives.

7 If stinger is still embedded, scrape it sideways from skin – avoid pinching or squeezing the venom sac.

8 Reassure and keep patient still and at rest.

9 Depending on the directions from EMS: a) clean the bite area with soap and water or rubbing alcohol, b) apply cold compress to area and elevate or c) apply a pressure immobilization bandage.

10 Transport to medical facility.

Patient Care – Coral, Jellyfish and Hydroid Stings

1 **STOP** – Assess and observe scene – *Is the patient still in the water? Is a venomous creature nearby?*

2 **THINK** – Consider your safety and form action plan – *How can I further protect myself and the patient?*

3 **ACT** – Check responsiveness and **ALERT** EMS, as appropriate.

4 Perform a primary assessment and monitor patient using the *Cycle of Care.*

5 If patient shows signs of a severe allergic reaction, treat appropriately. (See *Allergic Reactions* for more information.)

6 Once EMS is contacted, obtain and follow local medical control directions for field treatment prior to their arrival.

7 Reassure and keep patient still and at rest. Monitor patient using the *Cycle of Care.*

8 Treat jellyfish stings by liberally washing the affected area with vinegar (4-6 percent acetic acid solution) for at least 30 seconds to deactivate venom and prevent further envenomation.

9 After the stinging material (nematocysts) are removed or deactivated, the pain from the jellyfish stings should be treated with hot water immersion when possible. In the case of a major jellyfish sting, consider using pressure immobilization over the wound area after application of vinegar.

10 Transport to medical facility.

Patient Care – Octopus Bite and Cone Shell Sting

1 **STOP** – Assess and observe scene – *Is the patient still in the water?*
Is a venomous creature nearby?

2 **THINK** – Consider your safety and form action plan – *How can I further protect myself and the patient?*

3 **ACT** – Check responsiveness and **ALERT** EMS, as appropriate.

4 Perform a primary assessment and monitor patient using the *Cycle of Care.*

5 Once EMS is contacted, obtain and follow local medical control directions for field treatment prior to their arrival.

6 Reassure and keep patient still and at rest. Immediately place direct pressure on the wound with a sterile dressing, pad or gloved hand.

7 Apply a pressure immobilization bandage over the wound.

8 Transport to medical facility.

Patient Care – Fish Spine Injury

1 **STOP** – Assess and observe scene – *Is the patient still in the water?*
Is a venomous creature nearby?

2 **THINK** – Consider your safety and form action plan – *How can I further protect myself and the patient?*

3 **ACT** – Check responsiveness and **ALERT** EMS, as appropriate.

4 Perform a primary assessment and monitor patient using the *Cycle of Care.*

5 Once EMS is contacted, obtain and follow local medical control directions for field treatment prior to their arrival.

6 Reassure and keep patient still and at rest. Treat for shock if needed.

7 If needed, manage serious bleeding. If easily done, remove embedded fish spines.

8 Immerse wound in hot but not scalding water. Leave immersed for up to 90 minutes for pain relief. If needed repeat this treatment. If hot water does not provide pain relief, apply cold compress to the wound.

9 Clean wound with soap and water. Apply local antiseptics.

10 Seek medical assistance.

Emergency First Response®
Illness and Injury Assessment Record Sheet

▲ **STOP**– Assess and observe scene.

▲ **THINK** – Consider your safety and form action plan.

▲ **ACT** – Check responsiveness and **ALERT** EMS.
Treat patient in position found when safe to do so.

▲ **Perform a primary assessment and monitor patient using the**
Cycle of Care.

▲ **Explain Assessment Procedure to Patient – Wear Gloves if available.**

▲ **As you record information on this sheet for EMS, provide measured rates**
per minute and descriptive terminology.

Patient Information

Name _____

☐ Male ☐ Female   Date of Birth (Day/Mon/Yr) ____ / ____ / ____

Address _____

City _____ State/Province _____

Country _____ Zip/Postal Code _____ Phone _____

☐ Medical Alert Tag? Type _____

Patient Condition at Beginning of Emergency Responder Care

☐ Conscious ☐ Unconscious

Patient Position Prior to Care

☐ Standing ☐ Sitting ☐ Lying

To help guide your assessment, remember that:

◆ The average pulse rate for adults is between 60 and 80 beats per minute.

◆ The average pulse rate for children is between 70 and 150 beats per minute. Toddlers will be on the higher end of this average and older children will be on the lower side.

◆ The average pulse rate for infants is between 100 and 160 beats per minute.

◆ Average breathing rate for adults is between 12 and 20 breaths per minute. Patients who take less than eight breaths per minute, or more than 24 breaths per minute probably need immediate medical care.

◆ The average breathing rate for children is between 18 and 40 breaths per minute. Toddlers will be on the higher end of this average and older children will be on the lower side.

◆ The average breathing rate for infants (less than one year old) is between 30 and 60 breaths per minute.

◆ Average skin temperature is warm and skin should feel dry to the touch.

◆ Noticeable skin color changes may indicate heart, lung or circulation problems.

Summary – Primary and Secondary Care Provided

☐ CPR
☐ Defibrillation
☐ Serious Bleeding Management
☐ Shock Management
☐ Spinal Injury Management
☐ Conscious Choking Assistance
☐ Emergency Oxygen Use
☐ Illness Assessment
☐ Injury Assessment

☐ Bandaging
☐ Splinting
☐ Other _____

Patient Referred to:

☐ EMS Personnel   ☐ Hospital
☐ Personal Physician ☐ None
☐ Other _____

© Emergency First Response, Corp. 2011

Illness Assessment

SAMPLE – Signs and Symptoms

1. *How do you feel now?* _____

2. Patient's pulse rate _____ (use carotid or radial pulse; count beats for 30 seconds, multiply by two)

3. Describe patient's pulse: ☐ Rapid ☐ Strong ☐ Weak

4. Patient's respiration rate _____
   (count respirations for 30 seconds, multiply by two; avoid telling patient you are counting respirations.)

5. Patient's breathing is: ☐ Rapid ☐ Slow ☐ Labored ☐ Wheezing ☐ Gasping

6. Patient complains of: ☐ Shortness of breath ☐ Dizziness/Lightheadedness ☐ Chest pain ☐ Numbness ☐ Tingling in arms/legs

7. Patient's skin is: ☐ Warm ☐ Hot ☐ Cool ☐ Clammy ☐ Wet ☐ Very dry

8. Color of patient's skin is: ☐ Pale ☐ Ashen (gray) ☐ Red ☐ Blue ☐ Yellowish Blotches ☐ Black and Blue

sAMPLE – Allergies

1. Is the patient allergic to any foods, drugs, airborne matter, etc? ☐ Yes ☐ No

   If yes, what is he/patient allergic to? _____

2. Ask the patient if he has ingested or taken anything he may be allergic to: ☐ Yes ☐ No

3. Stung or bitten by organism? ☐ Yes ☐ No

saMPLE – Medications

1. Ask the patient: *Do you take medication?* ☐ Yes ☐ No

   If yes, *what type and name?* _____

2. Ask the patient: *Did you take your medication today?* ☐ Yes ☐ No

   If yes, *How much did you take and when?* _____

3. If possible, collect all medication to give to EMS personnel and/or get name of the doctor who prescribed the medication.

Illness Assessment (continued)

SAMPLE – Preexisting Medical Conditions

1. Ask the patient: *Do you have a preexisting medical condition?*   ☐ Yes   ☐ No

   If yes, *what type?* _____

SAMPLE – Last Meal

1. Ask the patient: *Did you eat recently?*   ☐ Yes   ☐ No

   If yes, *what did you eat?* _____

2. *What was eaten?* _____

SAMPLE – Events

1. Ask the patient: *What events led to your not feeling well?*   _____

2. *What were you doing when you began to feel ill?*   _____

3. *When did the first symptoms occur?*   _____

4. *Where were you when the first symptoms occurred?*   _____

5. Has the patient been exercising?   ☐ Yes   ☐ No

Attach additional Responder notes on separate sheet.

Injury Assessment

History _____

_____

What happened: _____

How did the injury happen? _____

When did the injury occur? _____

Injury Location (Follows Injury Assessment Order. Use Injury Key to denote condition.)

☐ Head _____
☐ Forehead, Cheeks, Chin _____
☐ Ears/Nose _____
☐ Tracking Eyes _____
☐ Pupils – Size _____
☐ Equal/Unequal _____
☐ Reaction to Light _____
☐ Skull, Neck _____
☐ Shoulder Blades _____
☐ Shoulders _____
☐ Collarbones _____
☐ Right Arm _____
☐ Right Hand _____
☐ Right Leg _____
☐ Left Arm _____
☐ Left Hand _____
☐ Rib cage _____
☐ Spinal Column _____
☐ Abdomen – Left/Right Side _____
☐ Hips _____
☐ Right Leg _____
☐ Right Foot _____
☐ Left Leg _____
☐ Left Foot _____

Injury Condition Key

A = Abrasion
B = Bleeding
Bu = Burns
C = Contusion (injury to tissues; no bone or skin broken)
D = Deformity
F = Fracture
L = Laceration (deep/jagged cut)
P = Pain
S = Swelling
T = Tenderness

Emergency Responder Care Given

_____

_____

_____

Additional Responder Notes

_____

_____

_____